MAKING CONNECTIONS WORK

The Young Adult's Guide to Getting a Job and Moving Up in the World of Work

By
**Edward Dejesus, Keith Hosea,
and Joseph Williams**

ISBN: 069285598X
ISBN 13: 9780692855980

Library of Congress Control Number: 2017904506

Publisher: Edward DeJesus Seminars and Consulting, Gaithersburg, MD

DEDICATIONS

Keith Hosea

This book is dedicated to my mother, Sharon K. Hosea. She was an extraordinary educator and a community leader. It is my privilege to continue her legacy.

Joseph Williams

Dakira, you are my world. Joseph, Capri and Zayla, you're my universe.

Edward DeJesus

Nicole, you are a never-ending source of love and the foundation of my strength. Candice, Cathy, Eddie, Elijah, Francis and Nicholas (wow, I got a lot of kids), you remind me why I work with other peoples' children – because I love you so much.

SUPPORTERS

We would like to thank the following individuals for their support of the Making Connections Work Indiegogo Campaign. Thank you for believing in us and the work we do.

Anthonie Jackson Sr.	Derrick Dolphin	Jaracus Copes
Elvis Diaz M.Ed.	Harold Aris	George Walcott
Shanequa Pannell	Leydis De La Cruz	Gregory A. Delts
Shelvee Casey	Adrienne Holloway	Natalie Lopes
Kyree Thompson	Donna Jonas	Eddie DeJesus
Katrina Bright	Maryanne I Graham	Lorenzo D. Harrison
Valerie Uccellani	Catherine DeJesus-Savas	Valarie Ashley
Damon Gaynair	Nora McDowell	Kendrick Lusk
Joseph Bilotta	Michael Gladfelter	John Conway
Victoria Dozier	Mr. G's Ice Cream	Edward Brantley
Chandika S. Johnson	Julie Lawson	Howard and Sheila Tate
Katherine Delaney	Reginald Glenn	Ruth Barajas
Dr. Jeshana Johnson	Sammy and Martha Acebal	James Rowen
Gregory Smith	Marina Streznewski	Nicole McCormack
John Ball	Daniel Peña	Jeffrey Zamoff

CONTENTS

PREFACE

When we were young, we thought that if we made enough money, we could go anywhere and do anything we wanted. Living in a capitalistic society, we assumed that money was the primary medium for getting things done, but we were wrong. We quickly learned through experience that we could earn money but still not have the credibility, the weight (or pull) to get what we wanted. There was something much more valuable, and no one gave us a clue how to get it—social capital.

Unlike money, you can spend social capital and never go broke. In fact, the more you spend, the more you make. This new formula for success wasn't taught to us in school or shared by others, including our parents. While our peers were paper chasing, we were social-capital canning—getting as many people as possible to know us and *like* us was the name of the game. And it worked. None of us ever had to look for a job in the traditional sense, and we all had our college and graduate-school education funded. We built pretty impressive careers for three brothers who only wanted to make a community better than the one in which we were born. If we could do it, you can too!

The idea of social and cultural capital was first introduced by a French sociologist named Pierre Bourdieu in the 1970s. Based on his observations, one of the key factors for young people's success was the value of their connections with others—social capital. Social capital, unlike financial capital, is easy to accumulate, and it grows exponentially. You don't need a business plan, high-interest rates, or the world's best stockbroker; you just need to be willing to invest some time in building relationships, establishing credibility, and doing unto others what you would want them to do unto you.

It's important to start social-capital canning as soon as possible. There are social-capital building opportunities all around you. Unfortunately, many adults don't realize its importance in a young person's life. They may create barriers of style, language, and culture that you must overcome, especially if you're from a different group. You must be responsible for building your social capital, especially if you're surrounded by adults who cannot.

When we think about it, every single job opportunity that we've been offered has been because we knew somebody! They didn't interview us because we had the perfect résumé or impressive credentials, the perfect amount of experience, background, knowledge, skills, and abilities. Not only did we know someone, but we knew someone who liked us. They went to bat for us, they referred us, and they recommended us. They pushed our applications to the top of the pile. They told us about job openings that had not been posted yet. They opened doors and called in favors and gave references that helped us get where we are today. In essence, that's the power of building social capital. We all need it. If you don't have it, you need to learn how to get it, and that's why we wrote this book.

Fifteen years ago, we came together, not to write a book but to build social capital. We knew that supporting, caring for, and helping each other grow would pay off in ways we couldn't even imagine. The publication of this book is just one example; the friendship we share is the rest.

Alive and free,

Keith Hosea, Joseph Williams, and Edward DeJesus

INTRODUCTION

In the next sixteen chapters, we will share the secrets to making strong workforce connections and the best ways to turn those connections into endless opportunities for success. *Making Connections Work* (*MCW*) is written for young adults, aged sixteen to twenty-four, who may be close to graduating from high school, community college, or a four-year university, and are anxious about finding a job or starting a career.

Making Connections Work is not about theory; it's about action. Each chapter contains three to six activities that will help you build the competencies needed to make and sustain strong workforce connections. By completing the activities in this book, you will see measurable gains in your job hunt and career-planning efforts. Successful adults have employed the techniques in this book for years, and it's time to teach these techniques to young people too.

Although most people find jobs through their personal connections, many schools don't train students in how to make them or support them in the process. At Social Capital Builders, we teach youth how to build and use this valuable asset to increase their future economic opportunity (FEO), and we actively work to support them in doing so.

The career success of adults contributes to the employment triumphs of youth. Your chances of hearing about job openings and vacancies increase exponentially when you are surrounded by gainfully employed adults. The more gainfully employed adults you know, the more your social capital grows.

At Social Capital Builders, we define social capital as the value of the social connections that exist between people. Unlike youth from impoverished communities where most of the adults are either unemployed or underemployed, young people from working-class communities have more opportunities to connect. That's if they're actively connecting or someone is trying to help them do so. Unfortunately, many youth with these types of connections rarely take advantage of them. It's usually because they weren't taught or supported in how to do so. If we added up all the unspent social capital, it would result in trillions of dollars in lost opportunities.

It's not enough to tell you that getting a job or education are the keys to success. That's like spitting in the wind. We may get it out, but the spit always comes back. Young adults are not dumb. You know it will take a series of developmental experiences, opportunities, and connections to ultimately attach to long-term labor-market success. If you don't realize it now, you will soon enough. What will you think about us then? What will you think when you realize a whole generation of adults withheld the truth about achieving economic success? The bonds of trust and reciprocation between the younger and older generations are eroding. Cracks have turned to craters. Soon they will be chasms that no one will be able to cross.

The majority of college graduates, 60 percent, can't find jobs commensurate with their degrees, and most will have fifteen to twenty jobs over the course of their working lives. That's a lifetime of mediocrity in an uncertain and changing economy. The traditional pathways of education and work are not leading the masses to the self-sufficiency promised land.

We tout the benefits of social media yet place little effort in helping you develop the social capital that built it. Social media is out of control and is now at a point where it hurts the average young job seeker more than it helps.

Every time we say job or education is the key to success without providing you with the additional supports necessary to build social capital, we are selling you short and further promoting the social inequality that many of us are fighting against.

As the right and left wage battle in the political and social landscapes, has it ever been more apparent that we need change? There is a glaring neon sign that says now is the time, but where do we start?

MCW is more than a book. It's a revolution. As we build social capital, we increase social justice. For far too long, too many have been left behind, even our own children. The failure to teach the importance of and invest in the development of social capital in schools and home is no laughing matter. It's the only way to stop the cracks.

Don't Leave It to Adults

Many people don't believe in the benefit of working hard to expand their circle of influence. Affluent young people learn these skills as a mandatory part of growing up. They witness the power of connection in their parents' alumni associations, business networks, and professional associations. Now is the time for every young person to learn these important skills and climb the ladder to success.

You must get out there and apply what you learn, attend events, make contacts, research, use connecting tools, and stay on top of your assignments. The difference between "networking" and "not working" is just one letter—*E*—and that stands for energy. Do you want a well-paying job? What about a job with upward mobility? A job that will take you places? A little *E* and a whole lot of connecting will get you there.

You may wonder, *What is future economic opportunity (FEO)?* At our firm, Social Capital Builders, we realize that the goal of building connections is not to get a job. In fact, a job will come easily. The years between sixteen and twenty-four are not wealth-building years; these are their FEO-building years. Every educator knows that a job is not the answer to success.

How many employed people do you know who are still broke?

Success is about acquiring the five elements of future economic opportunity and helping each and every young person acquire each of these elements, no matter what the costs. There is a big difference between a future economic-opportunity program and a job program. A job program is short-lived, and a future economic-opportunity program is long-term.

As a young adult between the ages of sixteen and twenty-four, your focus should be on making connections to develop your FEO and not simply on getting a job.

We define FEO as the acquisition of:

1. work experience
2. work-related skills
3. connections
4. industry-recognized credentials
5. educational degrees

Let's take a closer look at these five elements of FEO.

Work Experience

The acquisition of early work experience is the key to your future economic success. According to research conducted by Dr. Andy Sum, the director of the Center for Labor Market Studies at Northeastern University, early work experience strongly improves young workers' prospects for future success in the job market.

Beyond making sure that every youth can work, *Making Connections Work* focuses on helping you use your adult networks to:

1. uncover a variety of hidden work-experience opportunities (internships, externships, apprentice-ships, temporary, full-time, etc.);

2. help establish a documented work history and attendance;
3. connect with employers that will assist in securing future job opportunities;
4. secure documentable, high-quality references;
5. learn the skills, including "soft skills" that employers look for in successful employees; and
6. access information and support regarding union membership.

Skills

A skill is an acquired ability to do a task with expected results. Skill mastery does not take place in a classroom. It takes place on the job. The best way to learn a skill is to go out and do it, again and again. First, identify the skills you need to develop. The safest bet is to ask for help from someone who is established in a particular industry.

Information received from this group has proven to be more impactful and relevant than any other source of labor-market information.

The problem is that few people consciously share this information, and young people forget to ask. Despite formal connections to gainfully employed parents, mentors, and relatives, little sharing of the skills needed to be successful ever takes place. Without this information, you're forced to rely on secondary sources, which, for the most part are outdated or ignorant of today's labor-market dynamics, challenges, and changes.

Our goal to make sure you utilize the power of connections to gain critical information about the skills needed for future labor-market success. We structure connection opportunities in a way that helps you understand:

1. the value and transferability of the skills you already possess
2. skills relevant to success in a particular industry
3. the methods of acquiring those skills
4. how to translate skills into job and career success

Connections

"It's not only what or who you know; it's who knows you and likes you!" Since out first book, MAKiN' iT, we've been sharing this message about workforce success. It is one of our most famous Universal Survival Laws. Now, in MCW, we zero in on what it will take to make and build this essential element of FEO. This book that will help you:

1. identify current personal and familial connections that can assist in the building of future economic opportunity
2. establish plans to develop your level of social capital with a diverse group of adults
3. understand the importance of building credibility and rapport and initiate gazelle-like enthusiasm for doing so

Industry-Recognized Credentials

The US Department of Labor's Bureau of Labor Statistics (BLS) reports that there will be a limited demand for college-educated workers over the next decade. However, there will be a need for individuals with postsecondary education credentials for high-paying jobs. Despite this, credentials are the least understood and most often overlooked postsecondary educational option.

We assist you in using your connections to:

1. help identify relevant credentials for labor-market success
2. translate the value of the credential to employment and career-building opportunities

Educational Degrees

Completion of high school and postsecondary education has a direct impact on your future economic earnings. Yet less than 50 percent of students who enter college graduate four years later, and the numbers get worse for students enrolled at community college. Given the high cost of education and the importance of degrees to future career success, great effort must be placed in not only getting students into college but also making sure they complete it.

Connections can be a great source of assistance and inspiration when it comes to achieving postsecondary educational success. We assist you in using your connections to:

1. understand the importance of completing educational goals
2. identify courses of study that meet current labor-market demands
3. support access to, and acquisition of, financial assistance and scholarships
4. identify current educational opportunities
5. create a plan to access and secure these opportunities

At no time the history has building social capital been so important. It will help you unlock doors to future economic opportunities that have been regulated to only a well-connected few. Now is the time to get started. Making Connections Work is the key.

THE TRUTH ABOUT CAREER SUCCESS

"Successful young adults don't chase jobs; jobs chase them."
~Edward DeJesus

Connection Corner, Deirdre, age 27.

I started seriously connecting in 2008 when I was 19 years old. I met a connect who opened my eyes to a whole new world, a new beginning. I learned what connecting meant and began to build my connecting skills. I learned to speak publically and build my confidence. My connection introduced me to someone who helped me get into Wilberforce University. Through connections, I have been introduced to people who helped me learn new skills and habits, taught me the importance of commitment, hard work, dedication, and never letting your circumstances or situation determine your future.

It's the number-one skill for success in job hunts and careers. It's a skill that most young people don't realize is important until their senior year of college or trade school, and, by then, it's too late.

The evidence is deafening—the facts are indisputable. We will present the data, support the facts, and give you a strategy that, if employed (excuse the pun), will connect you to the nebulae of networks where most careers are born.

Consider this: how much time have you

put into perfecting the right résumé, scouring websites for job openings, and entering the same information over and over into online job applications—only to never get a callback? If you're like most people, the answer is "too much."

There's a secret known to only a few, and now you're one of them: successful young adults don't find jobs; jobs find them. The success of your job hunt and career-building efforts will rest mainly on turning contacts into connections and putting those connections to work for you.

Each year millions of job seekers follow the same ineffective strategy and get the same results—no job—or they spend a long time finding a job. We suspect that you are not one of these insane people. That's why you're reading this book. You want a fair shot at opportunity, and God knows you deserve one.

Someone once said, "Opportunities are never lost; someone will take the one you miss." Ask yourself this question, and give an honest answer: In the past year, how many opportunities have you missed? Each time you choose not to make connections with that professor, teacher, business-person, coach, mentor, and so on, who comes into your life, you let an opportunity slip through your fingers. It's like putting gold coins in a pocket full of holes. Although the coins fall through, someone else will pick them up.

It's truly unfathomable how many young people let these opportunities slip away, especially in a time of great economic challenge. More importantly, it's inexcusable that educational institutions have not made making connections a formal part of the curriculum. Too many young people miss out on economic opportunities because they aren't provided with the support to develop this key skill. The youth-employment rate is at its worst since the Great Depression, and college graduates lucky enough to find jobs are receiving wages that are 7 to 8 percent lower than those offered to graduates during healthier economic times. It's time to sew up your pockets and make sure you don't lose another gold coin.

We'll give you a solid plan to build your connecting skills and a strategy to implement them. We will refer to connecting, not networking. Although the term networking has been the buzz for many years, it has been abused over the last decade. For many, networking is simply about collecting as many business cards, Facebook friends, and social-media followers as possible. For others, it's about doing something for others so that they will do something in return. In our book, that's not a relationship; that's a transaction.

In fact, connecting is so much more. We define "connecting" as the cultivation of productive relationships for employment, educational, career, or business purposes.

How often have you seen people accumulate a stack of business cards or a googol of Facebook friends and never communicate directly with them again? Is this you? We know it's not that you don't care; it's that you're busy and have a ton of things on your plate. After all, you're looking for a job, right? (Hopefully a well-paying one with excellent benefits and tons of room for growth.) How can you look for work and stay in contact with all these people?

We know that it's not about quantity; it's about quality. It's not the number of people in your network; it's the number you cultivate into productive, mutually beneficial relationships that counts.

"I just want to get a job!" Don't worry, we hear you. We'll help you do that, but we'll also give you so much more. We'll show you how to open the door to hidden opportunities for long-term career success and future economic self-sufficiency.

Are you ready?

While most job developers and employment specialists are

adroit at explaining how to navigate the conventional job-search process, it's not the way the majority of people find jobs. Why would you spend a disproportionate amount of time on a process that doesn't work in your favor? Sure, some people get jobs through the conventional process, but guess what? Not many do. You have the facts, and you can prove it!

There are five main ways to find and secure a job:

1. connecting
2. agencies/recruiters
3. direct approach
4. Internet job boards
5. newspapers/periodicals

Let's take a closer look at each one of these sources.

Connecting

The use of a supportive system of shared information and services among individuals and groups with common interests to get, keep and progress in a job or career.

Staffing Agency/Recruiter

The use of a private or public service that acts as a liaison between employers and job seekers. A staffing agency collects, maintains, and manages thousands of resumes and matches them with prospective employers.

Direct Approach

The process of contacting hiring managers directly in order to get a job or advance in a career.

Internet Job Board

The use of a website or a nonvirtual posting board that facilitates job hunting. Users can typically deposit their résumés and submit them to potential employers, while employers can post job ads and search for promising candidates. The top job boards are Indeed, CareerBuilder, Monster.com, HotJobs, and Simply Hired.

Newspapers/Periodicals

A collection of job postings submitted by employers interested in fulfilling a specific job within a specific geographical area.

From 2008 to 2012, the Right Management Group, a global leader in workforce management and a consultant to 80 percent of Fortune-500 companies, conducted a study of how people find jobs (Marrow, 2013). About forty-seven thousand people were surveyed. Here are the results: Connecting has led people to as many jobs as the next three methods combined.

Right Management Group
Source of New Jobs Survey

Source	2012	2011	2010	2009	2008
Networking	46%	45%	47%	48%	41%
Agency/Recruiter	14%	13%	10%	9%	12%
Direct Approach	7%	7%	8%	8%	9%
Internet/Job Board	25%	26%	24%	19%	19%
Newspaper	1%	1%	2%	6%	7%
Other	7%	8%	9%	12%	12%

Numerous recent studies of how people get jobs confirm these finding even to the present day. Connecting trumps all other forms of job search. It does now and will do so far into the future. So where do you think you should invest your time? But why trust someone else's data when you have your own? Speak to five gainfully employed adults you know and complete the form on the following page.

GO TO WORK

Conduct your own survey. Speak to ten people with satisfying, careers. Ask them about the source of the jobs. Fill in the boxes below.
In the second box, calculate the totals and percentages. How do they compare to the national survey? What does this activity teach you about how people in your network find jobs?

Person	Company/Position	Source*
1.		
2.		
3.		
4.		
5.		
6.		
7.		
8.		
9.		
10.		

*Sources	Totals	%
Connection		
Agency/Recruiter		
Direct Approach		
Internet/Job Board		
Newspaper		
Other		

What did you learn about how people in your network find jobs? Are your findings consistent with the research? We've done this activity with hundreds of job seekers, both young and mature, and the answers are always the same. About 45 to 80 percent of people find jobs through networking. So where should you place your job-hunt and career-building efforts?

This might be a good time to share this information with your peers. Why keep it to yourself? In fact, you can use this activity to make a connection with adults. It's a great conversation starter.

> *"Mr. Smith, I'm doing some research about how people find jobs. Would you mind if I ask how you got your last three jobs? I want to compare your answers against the results of a national survey."*

The bottom line is this: if the majority of people in your network got jobs through connecting, then what are you waiting for?

We recommend the following breakdown for your job-hunt/career-development search:

- 50 percent of your time should be spent effectively making and building connections
- 20 percent of your time should be spent on Internet job boards
- 12.5 percent should be spent using the services of a recruiter/agency
- 12.5 percent should be spent on contacting employers directly
- 5 percent should be spent on scanning newspapers

We're not saying you should throw out the other sources—of course not. However, we are asking you to reexamine traditional job-search techniques. Consider placing the majority of your time and energy into making and sustaining workforce connections, and you will have a chance at staying on top of the economic changes that are rapidly restructuring our economy and the way people work.

HIDDEN JOBS AND
WHY YOU MUST FIND THEM

*"First, you have to be visible in the community. You have to
get out there and connect with people. It's not called net-sitting
or net-eating. It's called networking. You have to work at it."*
~Dr. Ivan Misner

Hidden Jobs

The majority of jobs are not posted in newspapers; they don't appear on job boards or on the Internet. They exist in what economists call the hidden labor market. In the hidden labor market, your success in getting a job is not based on what you know or who you know; it's based on who knows you and likes you. Various research reports state that between 40 and 80 percent of jobs are hidden.

But it doesn't stop there. The Right Management survey found that 44 percent of respondents think "who you know" is what determines advancement, while just 39 percent think it's job performance. For 4 percent, it's job tenure, and another 13 percent say they have no idea since their employer never provides clear criteria The bottom line is, your success in not only getting a job but moving up in the world of work is contingent on your connections.

What the Government Says

If you still aren't convinced that the hidden job market exists or that you don't need to implement our strategy to effectively job hunt and career build, let's take a look at a major government source—the Bureau of Labor Statistics (BLS). BLS is the principal fact-finding agency for the federal government in the broad field of labor economics and statistics. Each month, BLS releases the "Job Opening and Labor Turnover Survey," commonly called JOLTS. (I know it sounds like an energy drink, but this data should put some pep in your step to start our program.) JOLTS provides economists a snapshot of workers moving in and out of jobs, as well as jobs that go unfilled.

Each month, JOLTS tracks the number of hires that were made. It also tracks the number of advertised openings. The number of hires is always significantly higher than the number of openings. Employers are always hiring more people than claimed. This gap, usually between 38 to 40 percent, falls into the category of the hidden or unpublicized job market. There are always more hires than open positions, meaning that many positions that get filled are never advertised to the public. Where do these jobs come from? Outer space? The really important question is how do you get them?

This percentage has been consistent since JOLTS was instituted in 2002. Before that time, there was no record of hidden jobs. In conclusion, the hidden job market is real, but good luck in finding it.

Let's face it—times are tough, and many human-resources departments don't have the people power to deal with hundreds of résumés, especially when there is a more productive way of finding qualified applicants. Of course, certain positions with government agencies have certain posting requirements, but most private companies do not. Although it might seem like a good management practice, it is one that is easily circumvented to avoid the drama of five thousand applications for one job. Even if most companies have some standard policy of posting jobs, it's one that they rarely follow.

Cutting costs is the name of today's game, and companies are doing it by relying less and less on search firms and agencies. Why pay 15 percent of someone's salary to a search agency when you can find a more qualified candidate through internal company networking efforts?

Company secrecy is another major factor that promotes the existence of hidden jobs. Publically announcing new positions may reveal a company's plan for expansion or the launch of a new product line or service. Recruiting quietly through self-contained networks is far less risky than public advertisement is. The problem for most job seekers is that they are rarely in the know because they are not part of the network.

Why You Must Find Hidden Jobs

There are many reasons why you should work diligently to make connections. Research shows that employees hired through connections:

1. get hired faster
2. get better pay
3. stay on the job longer
4. have greater job satisfaction
5. enjoy greater benefits

Let's take at what our research at Social Capital Builders revealed about each of these areas.

1. Get Hired Faster

It's simple: employers trust their current employees more than they trust your online application. In fact, research states that employers tend to distrust sources of information outside of their own networks. In many cases, employers consider recommendations from teachers and job developers as suspect and prefer to rely on recommendations from known sources, such as current employees, when hiring workers. Current employees would not risk referring someone who

Connection Corner, Kevin, age 25.

We were just sitting around talking when my friend, Shane, mentioned that there was an opening at his company that management was having a hard time trying to fill. The funny part was I applied for that position twice and never got a response. Four years of college seemed like a waste. Later that week, Shane told me to come in. I met his director, and I was called in for an interview. The interviewer had the nerve to ask me why I didn't tell Shane I was looking for work. I felt like an idiot. I learned my lesson about the power of connections.

would make them look bad. If you want to get hired quickly, go through a referral, not a job board.

Employers are greatly concerned about how quickly they fill an open position. In human-resources jargon, it's called "time to hire." There's a high cost of finding the right person. Recruiting alone can cost companies thousands of dollars, especially if for low- to mid-level positions. The cost of advertisement; time cost for recruitment staff; interviews; and drug screens, background checks, and various pre-employment-assessment tests can wreak havoc on a company's bottom line. Do you think a manager wants to go through one hundred candidates or cut to the chase by accepting a referral from a long-standing, trusted employee?

A 2012 *Wall Street Journal* article stated that, on average, companies pay $3,500 in recruiting cost per employee. Many companies are looking to cut costs, and getting internal employee referrals is one of the best cost-cutting mechanisms around.

2. Get Better Pay

If you are referred through a connection, it probably means that you have inside information about what the company is paying and the salary you should request. Without this information, you're left to guess or leave it up to breaking the code of "pay commensurate with experience." It has been standard career-coaching protocol to advise job seekers to never ask about salary on the first or second interview, and, given today's tight job market, that advice might well extend into the fourth, fifth, and fifth job interviews. The problem with this approach is that you are flying without a flight plan and leaving it up to the employer to lay out salary parameters.

What if you had inside information? How could you use this information to help your career search? For starters, you would have a better sense of whether or not to even apply for the job. Maybe your Connect tells you, "The last person in that position made no more than forty K, and I doubt they will pay you more." Then you have some good information. If you are looking for sixty thousand, then you can save that energy for another employer. After all, have you seen the price of gas lately? Who has the resources to run to six job interviews with the same employer only to find out the salary is nowhere near what you desire? Moreover, the money you spend on transportation further reduces the salary that you don't want.

Millions of job seekers go into the job-hunt process with inside information about salary and benefits—information that career advisors tell you not to discuss till you get an offer. Don't wait till the offer to get the inside scoop; get connected now.

3. Stay on the Job Longer

Research shows that people who have been personally referred for a job stay longer on the job than those recruited through any other source (Sullivan 2015). Once again, it comes back to the person who referred you for the job. By knowing someone on the job, you get a more accurate portrayal of the work environment, work responsibilities, corporate culture, and the personalities of the people you are about to work with. Without this information, you rely on the job description and whatever you can discern during your six interviews.

Employers know this is important information. If recruitment costs give employers a headache, turnover costs are heart attacks. For example, sources estimate that turnover costs account for 30 to 50 percent of the annual salary of entry-level employees, 150 percent of middle-level employees, and up to 400 percent for specialized, high-level employees.

The longer an employee stays on the job, the better for the employer. The more connected you are to people in the workplace, the more likely you will stay on the job. It's a win-win situation for both you and the employer. Connections work in more ways than one.

We hope that by now you're getting our drift and are willing to invest fifteen minutes a day to making connections work. Just in case you're not convinced, we're going to continue.

4. Have Greater Job Satisfaction

Research shows a solid relationship between social networks and job satisfaction. Social networks affect job satisfaction by providing employees a sense of support. We aren't only talking about pats on the back. A supportive network in the company means you have a group of people to go to lunch with and also translates into something greater. You have access to information about new company developments well before the staff meeting and people to support you through difficult times.

Opportunity Costs That You Can't Afford

After thirty years in the field of workforce development, we were surprised and disheartened to discover that this information was not shared with students in a significant way. Instead, when seeking job-search assistance, most youth are given instruction on basic strategies such as handshake techniques and the best ways to answer the ten commonly asked interview questions. Of the hundreds of agencies we've worked with, not one took it to another level to train job seekers on how to build a network or supported them in doing so.

Making Connections Work was created to make sure every young adult has the truth about the job hunt and career success, no matter what their economic status.

As workforce-development experts, we've heard countless belabored tales of fear and confusion. Young adults describe how they spent valuable time and money on education and training, only to find out that the credential they received had little value in the open job market. Many felt betrayed. They felt robbed of resources and time. And we all know time is money. It's called opportunity costs—the cost of doing something better. Let's say that you have to study for a big midterm, but you've been invited to a concert. If you decide to study instead of attending the performance, the opportunity cost of studying is the enjoyment of being at the performance.

Let's give another example. Mark is about to graduate from college and is unsure about his career. He needs a job to start paying back student loans. Mark starts the process by writing a résumé, filling out one hundred online job applications, and going on ten interviews. At the same time, he hears about our program. He is told that by spending six hours a week building and sustaining connections, he will never have to search for a job again. A job will find him. He doesn't believe it and continues sending out résumés.

If Mark decides to continue his traditional job-hunt strategy instead of building connections, the opportunity cost of job hunting is the potential benefit of building more social capital.

"But Mark needs a job!" We hear you. Filling out online applications seems important to you; it's what you been trained to do. But building connections with gainfully employed adults is also critical. Both are important; however, let's be clear that what you're "losing" by traditional job hunting is an opportunity cost—a huge one. Not only will making connections help you find a job, but it will also set in motion a process to make sure you're never without a job again. The lost opportunity is the price for following traditional ways. In this case, you pay the potential of building a strong network. It's a costly mistake, and one the affects millions of young adults each year.

During the time of the terrible recession, more than three million well-paying American jobs from a variety of large and small employers remained vacant. While competition for so-called white- and blue-collar jobs is fierce, with candidates far outnumbering available positions, employers are still struggling to find Americans equipped with the skills and competencies needed to perform these jobs. Why? They don't know about you! You just put your résumé in with five thousand others. Employers cannot possibly do justice to that many applications coming in each week, no matter what the size of their HR department. The truth is, most well-run companies throw their formal recruiting process out the window when it comes to hiring the right candidate. Instead, companies turn to internal networks for the best candidate for the job.

What if you spent that time building strong connections with twenty-four gainfully employed people? Hundreds of thousands of smart job seekers bypass the traditional hiring process and connect their ways to jobs each year. Believe us, it works! But it won't happen to you unless you're connected.

Let's be honest—the conventional job-search process is not your friend. Anyone who tells you so is not being honest. Yes, having a résumé and cover letter are necessary evils, but that is less than 10 percent of the game. If you are relying on résumés, cover letters, and Internet job boards, you need to have your head examined. Someone lied, and it wasn't us. The traditional job-search process is all about finding ways to screen you out rather than welcome you in. Résumés are about your past; our process is about your future. Unless you have a 4.0 GPA, stellar work experience at a Fortune-500 company, and a working knowledge of the most sophisticated computer programs, you are asking to be screened right out of the process.

For years, we worked with underfunded schools serving young people who faced several barriers to employment. Most of the young people they served lacked real work experience and read well below grade level, and a few had criminal records. Do you think a résumé and the traditional job-search process helped these young adults find jobs? Seriously? It was just used as a tool to screen them out of a job, not welcome them in. The sad thing is that most schools don't realize this is just an insidious cycle. A cycle that goes like this: young people go out, submit tons of résumés and applications, and never get a callback. They become discouraged, disillusioned, and disconnected. They lose faith in the process and in the schools that have led them there. As a result, they disengage. This vicious cycle keeps many young adults disconnected from the labor market and educational institutions from meeting any significant measure of success. Without this evidence of success, schools are unable to make a case for increased funding—and the process starts all over again, this time with fewer young people served.

Not enough? Let's take a look at a college senior in a rough economy—hundreds of thousands of jobs are being lost each month, companies are closing their doors, and fewer jobs are available. Moreover, millions of résumés are flooding the job market. Even the elderly who once sought early retirement are being forced to work well past seventy just to make ends meet. The competition is fierce, and all you have is your résumé!

We've seen hundreds of young people get so frustrated with the traditional job-search process that they give up. They take the $8.25 per hour job just because they think they have to.

Today's labor-force-participation rate for young adults, the rate that takes into account the number of job seekers who have given up looking for work, is the lowest it's been since 1972. So many young people are giving up their job searches because they weren't taught the right way to look for work in the first place.

The traditional job-search process is not working and is leaving many out in the cold. Regrettably, someone else with less education and fewer credentials is getting employed, not by flooding the market with résumés, but by connecting their way to opportunity.

Our process is all about you. It's the smart way to look for a job and build your career. You become the face in front of the résumé, not the résumé hiding the face. You get the inside information on the jobs, promotions, and career-building opportunities. The process works; you just have to work it. It understands that actions speak louder than words, and we hope you are ready to get loud.

CHAPTER THREE

THE ART OF MAKING CONNECTIONS

"Social capital isn't scarce; your vision is."
~ Joseph Williams

Despite the facts we presented in the last chapter, many young adults don't take the time to build and sustain a strong network of people who can help them navigate a pathway to career success. They don't realize the value of social capital, and they don't invest in it. In reality, most adults don't either. Maybe they just don't believe the research, or they think that everyone who makes it simply did it on their own. One thing we learned is that from Bill Gates to Michael Jordan, no one makes it on their own.

Some young adults may believe in the benefit of expanding their circle of influence but don't feel like working hard at it. Sometimes they think they don't know enough people, or that few people would want to help.

In our work with hundreds of young adults, we have discovered an interesting fact. Few had to go outside their connections to find career and job opportunities. The people you need are probably just a phone call or visit away. You already know the person who is going to help you get your next job. The challenge is to act like it.

We hear so much about positive youth development and the importance of looking at young people as assets. If this is true, then why not start with the assets young people have in their own back pockets? Those assets are their internal connections.

In our program, we spend a lot of time helping students reflect on who they already know who can help them build FEO. We assist them in reconnecting with those people and in building strong bridges for career success.

We are often surprised by how many young people are directly or indirectly connected to company presidents and even local elected officials. In most cases, young people are less than three degrees from an influential person who can make a big difference in their careers. Our observations agree with the Small World Experiment in 1967, done by American psychologist Stanley Milgram (later to be known as the Six Degrees of Separation theory). This theory states that everyone and everything is six or fewer steps away, by way of introduction, from any other person in the world.

We are not saying that making connections will be easy. However, you are closer to your connection than you realize. It will still be work, but so is filling out one hundred applications and submitting one hundred résumés. The difference is that this work will have an immediate payoff and give you long-term dividends.

You probably have tons of friends whose parents could be beneficial to your success, but you don't even know their occupations. Your neighbors and other people you have known for years and come into contact with daily could all be sources to build your connections. It's time to put on your investigative hat and get some answers. It's pretty simple. Just ask.

Let's get started. The foundation of our process is building a cohort of twenty-four people you know who can help you in your career journey. Identifying these individuals begins with knowing why you want to connect with them. First, let's identify your specific FEO goals. Make sure your goals are things you can quantify and measure. They should be short-term goals, things that can be accomplished over the next three to twelve months. Remember, a future economic opportunity focuses efforts on long-term economic opportunity rather than temporary job placement. Having an FEO focus will help you be clear about what you want out of your connections and how they can assist you. Defining these goals will help you identify people in your network who will be beneficial in helping you reach them.

Here are a few examples in each of the five FEO areas.

Certification/Credentials

- I want to get my sigma-six certification.
- I would like to find someone who can help me pay for my real-estate license.
- I want to get government security clearance.

Work Experience

- I would like work experience in the field of health-care administration.

Connections/Social Capital

- I would like to meet someone who can serve as a mentor/advisor in the field of finance.
- I want to be mentored by a corporate CEO.

Degrees

- I would like to get a scholarship to help me pay for graduate school.
- I would like to meet a faculty member at a major graduate school.

Skills

- I would like to learn how to build and maintain websites.

- I would like to learn public-speaking skills from a professional.
- I would like to learn the skill of fundraising for nonprofits.

Next, think about the people you know who can help you reach these goals. Family friends, neighbors, former teachers—consider anyone who can help you reach your immediate FEO goal. Here is a list to help trigger some names. Don't stop until you have twenty-four listed. Don't worry about getting the contact information at this point. Just make sure that you do a thorough brainstorm of people in your network. We will cover the specifics about what information you should collect, how to collect it, and what to do with it later.

Politician	College Student	Musician
Community Leader	Store Manager	Lifeguard
Minister, Pastor, or Priest	Computer Phone Repair	Golfer
Celebrity	Working Dad	Soccer Player
Business Owner	Working Mom	Old Boss
Teacher	The Person No One Talks To	Construction Worker
Doctor	Therapist	Hairdresser
Dentist	Professor	Waiter or Waitress
Financial Advisor	Activist	Former Principal
Police Officer	Artist	Friend on Facebook
Lawyer	Ex-Boyfriend/Girlfriend	Uncle
Judge	Social Worker	Car Salesperson
IT Specialist	Counselor	Principal
Flight Attendant	Chef	State Worker
Correction Officer	Federal Employee	Family Member
City Worker	Banker	

We have found this activity to be extremely impactful in helping job seekers realize the power right in their hands. After you identify twenty-four people, rank your level of interaction with them regarding your specific career goal. Use the rating sheet on the next page. Mark a one if you never speak to your contact about your FEO goals or a ten if you frequently speak to that person about your goals. We are often surprised by the people our students know but have never spoken with about their career goals and plans for the future, let alone ask for help.

On a separate sheet of paper, let's do some future thinking. For each person, answer these questions:

- If you had fifteen minutes with that person, what would you speak about? For example: I would speak to Mr. Smith about how to get an IT job at a defense contractor or learn more about six-sigma certification.
- What do you think the impact of that conversation would be? WIth just a little conversation and some follow-up, the world of opportunity can be yours.

Complete the table below before moving forward.

MY CONNECT COHORT

In the past six months, how often have you spoken with your connects about your FEO goals?

CONNECTIONS	Never— — — — — — — — — — — — — — — — — — —Frequently									
	1	2	3	4	5	6	7	8	9	10
	1	2	3	4	5	6	7	8	9	10
	1	2	3	4	5	6	7	8	9	10
	1	2	3	4	5	6	7	8	9	10
	1	2	3	4	5	6	7	8	9	10
	1	2	3	4	5	6	7	8	9	10
	1	2	3	4	5	6	7	8	9	10
	1	2	3	4	5	6	7	8	9	10
	1	2	3	4	5	6	7	8	9	10
	1	2	3	4	5	6	7	8	9	10
	1	2	3	4	5	6	7	8	9	10
	1	2	3	4	5	6	7	8	9	10
	1	2	3	4	5	6	7	8	9	10
	1	2	3	4	5	6	7	8	9	10
	1	2	3	4	5	6	7	8	9	10
	1	2	3	4	5	6	7	8	9	10
	1	2	3	4	5	6	7	8	9	10
	1	2	3	4	5	6	7	8	9	10
	1	2	3	4	5	6	7	8	9	10
	1	2	3	4	5	6	7	8	9	10
	1	2	3	4	5	6	7	8	9	10
	1	2	3	4	5	6	7	8	9	10
	1	2	3	4	5	6	7	8	9	10
	1	2	3	4	5	6	7	8	9	10

Let's do some calculations. How many people were you able to list? Ten? Twenty? The full twenty-four? Based on a Columbia University study, the average person is connected to 611 people (McCormick TH, Salganik MJ, Zheng T, 2010). So coming up with 24 names shouldn't have been that difficult; that's only 4 percent of the people you really know. If you had difficulty listing 24 people, it means you didn't put enough effort into the activity. Stop here and go back and brainstorm the 24 gainfully employed adults in your life. Ask for help from a family member, if you need to.

Now here comes the real question. What was your average frequency of contact with these connections? To figure this out, add up the individual ratings given to each connect and divide that number by the total number listed. We call this the connection quotient (CQ). For example, let's say you rated your connection frequency a five for the first twelve connects, and an eight for the remainder.

$$(5 \times 15) + (8 \times 12) = 156/24 = 6.5 \ (65 \ percent)$$

If your CQ is under 60 percent, you need to ask yourself, "Am I serious about getting a good job and/or building a career?"

In light of the information we've shared so far, you may be putting the right effort into the wrong strategy. We hear countless stories of people who completed fifty or more applications only to never get a job, yet their CQ is consistently less than 40 percent.

Remember our recommendation for how to go about a job/career search:

- 50 percent of your time should be spent effectively making and building connections
- 20 percent on Internet job boards
- 12.5 percent using the services of a recruiter/agency
- 12.5 percent on or contacting employers directly
- 5 percent on Newspapers/periodicals

Your Weak Ties and Strong Ties

Here's some good news. Each one of the people on your list is likely to know someone else who might be interested in lending you support. Based on classic research by Dr. Mark

Granovetter, a Stanford University professor, 60 percent of workers find out about their jobs through personal contacts, yet the majority of these personal contacts are people they did not know well. He called these weak ties. Granovetter found that uncovering the strength of weak ties in job searches is more helpful in landing jobs than using one's close friends (Granovetter, 1974).

Granovetter makes a case against one's immediate network by suggesting that close friends often introduce job seekers to familiar jobs, whereas weak ties connect them to ones that they may be unfamiliar with or may even be unaware that they exist.

As a young adult, you probably have not invested a whole lot of time building connections with strong ties—that's why you're reading this book. Asking you to focus on another group, weak ties, may seem overwhelming. Don't worry. Later in the book, we'll give you a strategy to develop both simply and easily, all in one easy task.

To help you along, we break it down like this:

A *strong tie* is an individual you know on a first-name basis, whom you see frequently and who can help you with your career goal.

A *weak tie* is an individual your strong tie knows on a first-name basis, with whom you have infrequent contact or casual relations and who can help you with your career goal.

Now guess what? Each of those twenty-four people you identified is a resource to help you build your weak-ties list. (*Note*: If you haven't completed the connect-cohort activity, we highly suggest you stop now and do it. As we said earlier, this is a process. In order to see benefits from it, you must work the process.)

Now we want you to take steps to start developing your weak-ties list. You will learn things that will help you gain the confidence and skills to build these connections. But right now, you can start to think about your weak ties and how they can be developed.

For each connect, use the weak-tie building activity below to help you brainstorm the possible weak-tie connections and how they can benefit you.

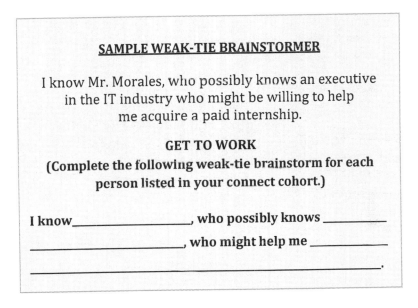

SAMPLE WEAK-TIE BRAINSTORMER

I know Mr. Morales, who possibly knows an executive in the IT industry who might be willing to help me acquire a paid internship.

GET TO WORK
(Complete the following weak-tie brainstorm for each person listed in your connect cohort.)

I know_____, who possibly knows _____
_____, who might help me _____
_____.

The Significance of Weak Ties

Many students find it difficult to identify strong ties, let alone come up with a potential list of weak ones. Weak ties are important and are sometimes a more effective source of opportunity referrals because they hold less bias against you than a strong tie does. For example, let's say that in your sophomore year of college, you were busted for smoking marijuana. Your neighbor, Mr. Morales, was made aware of your issue in a conversation with your mother. It has been three years since that incident, and Mr. Morales has seen you mature and take responsibility for your actions, and he knows you are about to graduate from college. For the past three years, your mother has been telling Mr. Morales how proud she is of you for getting a 3.6 GPA and helping out at the local homeless shelter. Although he has witnessed your transformation, somewhere deep in his mind, Mr. Morales may still be a little hesitant to give you a referral because of his familiarity with your experience. It's not that he won't help; he just has a natural bias against you. However, it is unlikely that he will communicate this bias about you to any of his strong ties (your weak ties). Consequently, getting assistance from someone he knows will probably be more helpful than getting assistance from Mr. Morales himself.

A noted sociologist, Sandra Smith, discovered a hesitation in people to refer close friends to jobs (Smith, 2015). She attributed this to two reasons: (1) people are concerned about the personal impact in the event the referral doesn't work out and (2) they were unsure whether or not the friends would work out due to their personal knowledge of their shortcomings.

Based on the work of these two well-respected researchers, we want you to work on building your weak-tie list. While you may have a plethora of connections to strong ties, don't discount the power of turning weak ties into strong ones and their role in helping your build your career.

Later on, we'll teach you techniques to build credibility with your strong ties as well as ways to get them to share ties to help you build FEO.

So take a moment to answer this question honestly. With all that we shared in the first few pages, what would you think of a program that would train you to build your *ties* and support you in doing so? Would you be willing to invest thirty minutes a day in this program?

THE PROBLEM MAKING CONNECTIONS

"Social capital shields good kids from their worst moments."
~ Edward DeJesus

This is perhaps the most significant question we ask during our workshops. "If people know the power of building social capital, why don't more people do it?" Why aren't more schools and programs teaching this important skill and supporting young people in it? We don't have the answers right now, but we do have some theories.

Whatever the reason, you can't let this hold you back. The economy is in shambles, and you have invested both time and money in a good education or credentialing program. You're on a mission to get yourself a career-level job with good pay, room for advancement, and great benefits. You have no time to play around, dream, or drift.

The Barriers

We have encountered five major barriers that prevent young adults from fully engaging in the process. We continuously see them rear their ugly heads as we conduct programs throughout the United States. The even appear with adult job seekers who are desperately seeking to re-enter the world of work. These barriers are:

1. being unclear about what they want from a connection
2. being afraid to ask others for help

3. lacking time to make connections
4. using the excuse of being an introvert
5. being unsure who to connect with

Let's go through each of these.

1. Being unclear about what they want from a connection

Someone once said, "If you don't know what you want, you end up with a lot you don't want." Our program is not about wasting people's time. We don't want to waste yours. You have to be precise in what you want to get out of the connecting relationship and even clearer about what you are willing to put into it. Completing the book and engaging in the process will equip you with clarity of purpose that most connectors don't possess. We have started the process with you, but there is so much more to come.

2. Being afraid to ask others for help

At Social Capital Builders, we realize that most young people will feel strange and uncomfortable about making connections, so we train wingpeople (an adult, parents, or another graduate of the program) on the proper way to support them in doing so. For example, we advise wingpeople that during connecting events to reach out to the event organizer and introduce themselves and their young people, get a quick lay of the land, and ask for the names of several people with whom they should connect. It's that simple. You don't have to come up with a reason to connect; someone will always develop one for you. Just ask!

Here's an example. "Hi, Jim. My name is Ed. Brian suggested we come over and speak to you. He said you just opened a new business and are looking for ways to get the word out. How can I help?" Of course, you may not be an expert on business marketing, but you don't need to be. Let Jim tell you how you can help.

Connection Corner, Stacy, age 22.

I was a prolific procrastinator. I believed I worked best under pressure, but the truth was I never gave myself enough time to get the job done right. I always waited until the last minute to get things done. I was often rushed, performed an incomplete job, and frequently missed deadlines. I was employed part time at a community-based organization. The director entrusted me with several important tasks involving the recruitment and transportation planning for the company's annual youth conference. Two months before the event, he asked me to provide updates as to how things were coming with the recruitment process. I said everything was going well, but the truth was I had not started the project. I kept telling myself, "I can get it done tomorrow." One month before the event, the director called me into his office. He sat me down and asked directly, "Where are we with registrations for the event?" I broke down into tears and admitted that I barely started making calls. It was then that I realized that my procrastination habit had gone too far. I had to do something about it.

Here's another example. You're at a family event. Your mother shares with you that your cousin's husband is a construction manager at a major construction firm. Just go up and introduce yourself and ask, "Is there any way I can help? " You'll be amazed at the results.

Don't be afraid; people are wired to connect. Developing rapport is usually the first stage, and showing interest in others is the way to accomplish it. Once you do this, they will have no problems connecting with you.

3. Lacking time to network

Really? I want to throw a clock at you. We already talked about the five elements of FEO: skills, credentials, connections, degrees, and work experience.

I think you would agree that these things are important to your future success. However, values don't always equal actions. I'm an ironman triathlete. If I were

41

to tell you that I spend only three hours a week training, you'd know that I'm not an ironman triathlete. Maybe a sprint triathlete. That type of training will get me no closer to completing a 2.4-mile swim, a 114-mile bike ride, and a 26.2-mile run than doing one push-up a week will get me to Mr. Olympia.

Dr. Ivan Misner, who heads the world's largest networking organization, BNI, reports that successful connectors spend an average of six hours a week participating in connecting activities. Just to be clear, chatting with your friends on Facebook is not a connecting activity. In our process, we define connecting as any type of interaction that helps you establish rapport and credibility with people.

Given that this book is aimed at young adult ages sixteen to twenty-four, we're going to cut Dr. Misner's recommendation in half. Most of you don't have businesses that you're trying to grow or payrolls that you're trying to meet. Right now, it's all about building your FEO. In this case, you can reduce Dr. Misner's recommended amount of time and still see substantial gains from the process. That means we're talking about thirty-six minutes a day—that's it. Thirty-six minutes a day to build a bridge to a great job, a promising career, and untold fortunes.

You can decrease the amount of time once you get settled into a job unless you want to go full "connecting commando" and build a million-dollar corporation or social movement. With a minimum of thirty-six minutes a day, however, you can radically develop more positive opportunities in your life.

Do you have thirty-six minutes? At the beginning of an MCW session, we ask young people to identify their biggest time wasters—activities that do not contribute to their FEOs. What they come up with is amazing. It is glaringly obvious that more than thirty-six minutes a day is wasted on frivolous things that not only do not enhance FEO but take away from it. In almost all cases, young adults reach a turning point in their lives where they realize the costs of these time wasters and take immediate actions to curtail them. For some, it means discontinuing social-media accounts, letting go of friends, or selling gaming systems. In all cases, significant FEO gains are made when time wasters are eliminated. Tell us your biggest time waster story below.

Here are the biggest time wasters, based on a survey of one hundred young adults in our program:

- texting
- social media
- kickin' it (whatever that means)
- sleeping

Let's do yours.

Activity	Time per Day	Time per Week
Totals		

Based on your results, can you find thirty-six minutes a day to build your future?

Yes_____/No_____

4. Using the excuse of being an introvert

The misconception about networking is that you have to be an extrovert to be successful. I'm one of the biggest introverts you will ever meet. Despite being a public speaker, I dislike crowds, and groups exhaust me. When I finish speaking, I am usually so mentally drained that I need to work out or go to my hotel room and nap. I need to make sure I give myself time and space to unwind, even if it's a good swim in the pool at eleven at night.

Being an introvert is all about where you get your energy from, not who you give it to. For the majority of us, it comes from being alone, doing something we enjoy. For my co-authors, who have different personality types, this may not be a big issue. For the most part, much of the MCW process is nonverbal: sending and writing letters, notes, and e-mails. There will be some phone calls made, and attendance at only a few actual events required. We'd be surprised if you spend more than one hour each week at an event. When you do attend events, you will be armed with specific goals: the number of people to meet, YOUTRY statements to deliver, or connection cards to complete. When you accomplish your goal, it's time to say "see ya," and go and recover.

5. Being unsure who to connect with

You'll already know the majority of your connections. Don't worry. However, if you fall short, you may need to attend a few connection events. The key is to never go into a connecting event without a plan and a wingperson. The process is pretty simple: ask your wingperson to find the host of the event, get an introduction, and tell the person what you're trying to achieve. They will point you in the right direction. At Social Capital Builders, we train wingpersons to contact the host before the event to explain the goals of the program. Many people want to provide opportunities to benefit youth lives. Although you may not be enrolled in our program, we do suggest you find one. However, if there's not one in your area, take the initiative and start a chapter. Contact us at www.socialcapitalbuilders.com for details.

What are your barriers to making workforce connections? Take some time to think about them and possible solutions, and write them down in the spaces below:

Barriers to MWFC

Barrier/Challenge	Possible Solution

This exercise can help you kick off discussions with potential connects. You'll be surprised that most of your connects have dealt with similar issues over the course of their careers and probably have many helpful and relevant recommendations.

Most job seekers can overcome barriers to making connections with the assistance of a skilled wingperson. Wingpeople's support is not only about helping you make connections; they help you develop the skills, tools, and resources to effectively do so. A wingperson can help you make the right social capital investments that can lead to a lifetime of opportunity and achievement.

A well-trained wingperson is responsible for making sure the necessary resources and supports are in place for you to turn the skills you learn in MCW into real, viable opportunities for lifelong learning, long-lasting relationships, and future economic opportunity.

A wingperson is a/an:

- advisor
- mentor
- guide
- facilitator
- convener
- coach

Not all adults know how to assist youth in making connections. Many are unfamiliar with techniques or don't recognize the need to do so. At Social Capital Builders, we have developed a home-study course for adults who are interested in being wingpeople. They can find more about it by visiting our website at www.socialcaptialbuilders.com.

CHAPTER FIVE

SOCIAL CAPITAL AND BUILDING ADULT CULTURAL COMPETENCE

"Serve those who are where you want to be in life."
~ Joseph Williams

As consultants, we spend several days a year working with directors representing schools, foundations, and nonprofit organizations, trying to help them understand the importance of helping youth build social capital. We always start meetings with two key questions for each person present:

1. How do you use your financial capital to help students get jobs and build careers? The answers are always quick and witty: we can contribute, raise, and invest money. They talk about building new campus wings, funding new scholarships, and securing corporate support to help promote the sustainability of the school.

2. Then we ask, "How do you use your social capital to help your students get jobs and build careers?" There are always a few uneasy seconds of silence as they search the dark spaces of their hippocampuses for answers.

Financial capital is the accumulated material wealth (money, real estate, stocks) used to generate income or make an investment. With regard to the questions above, this definition is easily relatable to helping students succeed. After all, for most people, the contribution of financial capital is simply a matter of writing a check or transferring stock. However, the contribution of social capital is not as easy. Social capital is the value of the social connections that exist between people.

Connection Corner, Demetrius, Age 22

The best way to describe my first job search out of High School is one word: frustration. I applied to dozens of places; I stood in line with hundreds of applicants at places like Stater Bros. and Best Buy, only to be disappointed to find out I was not chosen for the job! I was recruited by scam artists who offered me high paying "management positions," only to find out they just wanted me to sell products door-to-door. Things changed after I learned about the hidden job market from one of my mentors. He took me to some of his meetings with his friends and business associates. He introduced me as his protégé, and the next thing I knew, some of these new acquaintances were asking me about what kind of work I wanted to do. In a matter of weeks, I was offered several jobs. It changed the way I think about looking for work and the value of relationships in reaching my personal goals.

A person connected to a Major League Baseball team-owner association tends to have more social capital than someone who is not, at least regarding access to baseball resources. The value of those connections is real and has much worth. Through these connections, that person has the opportunity to learn the language, culture, and expectations of the industry and opportunities within it. People without these connections will be required to fend for themselves, often relying on information from a book or website.

Similarly, a person with connections to business-owner associations has more social capital than one who doesn't, at least assuming that everything else remains constant.

The more connections you have to working individuals, the stronger your access to employment information and resources. Possessing timely and relevant labor-market information will be the key to helping you not only get a job but better prepare you for the type of well-paying job that you want to get.

Connecting requires respect for the cultures of both parties. Culture often affects the way people communicate. Learning to speak the language of others is a sign of respect and an overall desire to genuinely connect. If you fail to speak the language, or if they fail to hear yours, building a relationship will be difficult.

Accessing these individuals and establishing these connections will depend on your ability to speak their language and show deference to their culture. We're not talking about ethnicity (that's for another book). As people develop in their professions, they develop a unique set of values, behaviors, attitudes, mannerisms, and customs based on the type of industry and the majority of people in it. Plumbers, for the most part, celebrate the language of early to bed and early to rise whereas artists may speak something entirely different.

You can radically improve your chances of making connections by understanding the factors which contribute to the culture of work. Here are a few questions to research before making connections within certain industries:

- How do they conduct work?
- What are their behaviors and style?
- How do they use language?
- How do they problem-solve and deal with conflict?
- How do they negotiate?
- How do they develop relationships with others?

Social capital grows based on common connections and a shared language. Eric Lesser, the author of *Knowledge and Social Capital*, attributes one of the difficulties in transferring social capital to a lack of a common set of values and norms between different groups. According to Lesser, without this understanding, sharing becomes difficult (Lesser, 2011).

Take, for example, an inner-city school. While the board of

directors actively fights to raise money (financial capital), only a few members actively work to share social capital (the value of their networks) with the students in their program. Why? Many board members might think, *What interest would students have in being around my circle of friends and acquaintances? They would feel out of place and have no basis for a connection.* What the board members may fail to realize is that they are the basis for the connections, and it is this transference of social capital that can lead to great opportunities for students. In many cases, sharing social capital can benefit students and the outcomes of the program more than raising one hundred thousand dollars would.

For many young adults, especially those from less privileged backgrounds, lack of opportunity stems from the inability of the greater power structure to share and transfer social capital. More valuable than financial capital, social capital can be spent in acquiring information about, and access to, opportunities that have only been enjoyed by the well-networked few. We see this in many segregated communities. Low-income children do not have access to a wealth of information about jobs and careers and few examples of people in it. Without these examples and access, building a solid career plan becomes difficult.

Building Social Capital through Adult Cultural Competence.

In a world where there is a lack of understanding about the importance of social capital and an unwillingness to share it, you must take responsibility for accumulating it. It is ten times more powerful than financial capital in terms of eventual return on investment.

To build social capital quickly, you will have to take responsibility for developing and demonstrating an understanding of the common values and procedures of the groups you're trying to connect with. We call this adult cultural competence (ACC). At Social Capital Builders, we have built a career teaching educators how to relate and connect with youth successfully. We term this process youth cultural competence (YCC)— the process of using the elements of youth popular culture, peer influence, and youth involvement to reach youth with a message about the importance of education and workforce development. We have seen some incredible results when educators take the time to invest in strategies to better relate to youth and young adults.

However, this is not a one-sided equation. There is a reverse side that can be equally beneficial, if not more so. The process of connecting to adults and building shared interest is a less talked about strategy for workforce development and an even more important one. Exactly what is adult cultural competence, and how can one use it to advance career opportunities? Clearly, there is a distinction between youth culture and adult culture.

Adult Culture	Youth Culture
Conservative	Risk-Taking
Seeks Security	Seeks Opportunity
Linear Thought	Out-of-Box Thought
Consistent	Traditional

Let's define adult cultural competence (ACC) along a similar vein. ACC is the process of engaging adults, connecting to their values, and establishing credibility, all in an effort to promote your future economic opportunities and social capital.

When working with schools, we urge them to host a culture mixer. Unlike traditional cultural exchange events where groups bring in favorite ethnic foods and customs, the cultural mixers we promote urge adults to bring in items important to their cultural values and encourage youth to do the same. Both groups get an opportunity to share what they value and to engage the other group in an examination of that item. It is fun to see a young person sharing an example of a new Smartphone app, while an older adult brings in a stopwatch given to him by his grandfather. The exchange is priceless, and it leads to a greater understanding and appreciation for what both youth and adults bring to the table.

Too often this exchange is one-sided, with the adult taking responsibility for connecting with the youth. Unfortunately, in the real world, all youth turn into adults. It might be a better world if all adults turned into youth, but we don't think that's going to happen anytime soon. Understanding and relating to those who possess the keys to opportunity makes sense and is a necessary competence for all young job seekers.

While the recent growth of millionaires under the age of thirty has been fueled by the technology revolution, young people still only account for less than 1 percent of corporate CEOs. Building your ACC is an investment that will enable you to increase that percentage. Each adult you add as a connection can pay off exponentially.

The good news is that developing this competence is pretty easy. It just takes some work. It's a competence that time eventually forces you to develop. Think about it. How long did you wait till you bought that nice business suit? When did you say to yourself, "I need to get a real pair of dress shoes and stop trying to make it by with these Docksiders." When did you say: "OK, I got to cut these locks"? Oh yes, and you probably changed your e-mail name from ilikegirls@website.com to something much more conservative. Believe us; you will do all these things in due time. We're certain. Participation in the mainstream labor market demands it.

In schools across the nation, we do a little activity to prove our point.

Let's take it a little further. Adult cultural competence is not only about how you dress and your e-mail address. It goes much deeper than that. It often involves your perspective on the world and how you share it. Look at any hip-hop magazine. How many grimaces do you see? Now pick up a business magazine. Count the number of smiling faces in each. There is usually a one-to-five ratio of smiling faces to pages in the business magazine, and a one-to-thirty-seven ratio in the hip-hop magazine. Will Smith doesn't count.

What type of message does this type of portrayal send to adults about inner-city youths' interest in building connections? If making connections is the number-one way to jobs and economic opportunity, then this type of media portrayal is economic suicide. Moreover, it conditions youth to engage in insidious behaviors that undermine their future economic opportunity, all in the name of being cool. Not all inner-city youth walk around mean mugging, but way too many do. If everyone sees them as grimacing, they'll be scared of these and unwilling to connect with them.

It sounds simple, but it's not. We've traveled to more than sixty cities where we see young people adopting insidious actions, tools, beliefs, and behaviors that they think are helping them survive, but, in reality, all they do is undermine their lives, freedom, and future economic activity. We talk about this extensively in our first book, *MAKiN' iT*. You may not be living the codes of the streets, but the question you need to ask yourself is this: Which of my behaviors, actions, and values make building social capital difficult?

We spoke to several social-capital-building experts and found the following behaviors to be connection killers and major barriers to building social capital with adults.

Lateness

Are you late for everything? If so, that's a great way to ruin a connecting relationship. As stated earlier, your connects' time is precious. There is no reason to keep them waiting. They may have kept you waiting, but you should never keep them waiting. If you want someone to recommend you for a position or another form of opportunity, the last thing you want to put in their head is that you have problems with attendance and punctuality. Always arrive at least thirty minutes early to every event or meeting. Use those thirty minutes to work on your MCW process. That way you will have a purpose to arriving early and not feel that you are wasting time.

Complaining

We know the world is tough, and things aren't fair. However, your connects are not your counselors. They are there to help you move forward. The worst thing you can do is bog down precious time in wallows and sorrows. Focus on the positive. Share what you're doing to build FEO. Share your FEO portfolio and ask for suggestions. Never, ever talk badly about someone. Always keep the conversation positive and light.

Politics and Religion

Stay away from both. If you are Republican and your connect is a Democrat, who cares? Your goal is to build your FEO, not run for political office. Bringing up current events can be risky; that's why we want you to stay focused on your FEO. We have tons of questions to help you drive the conversation. There is no room for religion or politics in connecting.

If your connect nudges you in that direction, redirect quickly: "Mr. Jones, I really don't care much for politics. I was wondering, though, what do you feel is the best investment I can make in my personal development at this point of my career?"

Drinking

I attend tons of connecting events, and there is always wine and beer. If you are of age, is it a good idea to walk around with a beer in your hand or alcohol on your breath? The answer is absolutely no! A study by the University of Pennsylvania found that people who hold an alcoholic beverage are perceived to be less intelligent than those who do not. They call it the "imbibing idiot bias (Rick and Schweitzer, 2012)."

While you are sipping on the syrup, others are taking advantage of your mistakes and making those connections that you missed—not to mention the possibility of having your whole life ruined by a car accident or DUI. Leave the drinks alone.

Dress

The answer is always business casual. Please don't show up looking like Dennis Rodman at a Mardi Gras parade. For women, it is also about being conservative. Some people think connecting is about attracting attention. It's not. The revealing cleavage or tight dress is not the answer, and neither are the bright colors. Get attention by connecting well and more often.

We are not telling you these traits are exclusive to young people. Many adults have difficulty getting to work on time, displaying good attitudes, and so on. However, the important message is that you are the one trying to build your social capital so that you can spend it like cash later. You must be prepared to code-switch and live up to standards and expectations that you might have rejected in the past. At Social Capital Builders, we may not be able to teach you how to code, but we can sure teach you how to code-switch.

In the box below, list seven steps you can take to build your social capital. Share your list with adults in your network. Get their feedback and suggestions, and watch yourself build social capital in no time.

Get to Work: Seven Steps to Building Social Capital	
Steps	Feedback

A Special Message to Athletes

During your athletic career, you are taught numerous skills, such as how to catch or block for football, post up or dribble for basketball, or cradle for lacrosse. These skills have been ingrained in you through practice and repetition since Pop Warner or kids' leagues. Unfortunately, many young athletes are not taught an equally important skill—connecting. Whether it is in high school or college, you have more opportunities to connect than your academically focused peers. Like all public figures, you are easily recognized and held at a higher bar than other young adults. This status of popularity and exposure can give you a step ahead in the connecting realm. Using this step could prove to be instrumental if you are interested in heightening your career and/or job opportunities.

We all know the story of the high-school sports star with three different division-one offers. Many adults who are associated with the high school know this young adult and hold him or her in high regard. Athletes like this get more business cards and hear the line, "if you ever need anything...feel free to contact me," a lot more than their peers. Playing sports is one way to show adults that you possess dedication, discipline, competitiveness, and drive—all qualities desperately sought out by today's businesses.

Striving to be a professional athlete is a great pursuit, but also a competitive one. If you're not drafted or picked up by a professional team (and you most likely won't be), you are left at the same level as your peers if you don't use the dynamic network given to you by playing your respective sport.

Over your athletic career, you will meet many influential people who love to share their contact information. Don't take this contact information for granted. For the nonathlete masses, getting access to these influential people is almost impossible.

MCW should be mandatory reading for every young adult, including athletes, because it gives them a system to put these contacts to work for them. It helps them establish lifelong contacts that can mean the difference between the unemployment line and a career. Moreover, it goes further. It reminds athletes that they are public figures; anyone and everyone will know when you mess up. The high regard that adults hold for you can be tarnished in the blink of an eye by an inappropriate tweet or Facebook comment. Proper use of social media is of the utmost importance to athletes. The effective use of making connections is paramount.

CHAPTER SIX

CONNECTORS AND CONNECTS

"You already know the person who is going to help you get a job. Act like it!"

~ Edward DeJesus

There are many ways to connect to others in the world of work. Our process has proven to be effective and is an essential skill for job seekers who are serious about establishing their careers. Every productive person you meet is an asset. They can help connect you to jobs, other people, and important labor-market information and opportunities.

Certain tools will help you effectively build and maintain connections. A carpenter without a hammer isn't really a carpenter. It's the same with our process. You need tools to build connections. In this chapter, we'll take a look at some.

Our process is not only about connecting you to jobs. It's about connecting you to opportunities. It will not only lead you to employment, it will lead you to scholarships, contracts, and grants. It will help you get accepted into the best graduate school. It will provide you with the most relevant labor-market information to make good decisions about your career or calling. The benefits of making and sustaining connections are immeasurable. By increasing your connections, you are opening the doors to untold opportunities.

In essence, it's all about building social capital.

As stated earlier, 70 percent of jobs are found in the hidden labor market. Information about them is held by a select few.

Connection Corner, Jesse, Age 21

I met my connect in 2009, after gaining employment with a non-profit. I was young, and this was the second job I had obtained after graduating from high school. One of my personal goals in life was to grow as a professional. We would have bi-weekly meetings where he would talk to me about professional and personal growth. He showed me how to communicate effectively. I learned how to not only create goals but also build pathways to reach them. He taught me that to be successful, I had to push myself. I learned that a person needs to be approachable, sociable, and reliable. With those three skills, I began building a professional network of people that not only have helped me obtain jobs but assisted me in overcoming many obstacles. I realized that I became more than an individual; I become part of a team.

That's why we say, "The secret to getting a good job isn't only what you know, or who you know; it's who knows you and likes you!" In this chapter, we'll start developing the skills needed to break into this circle of weak ties.

In the process, there are two types of people: the connector and the connect.

A connector is a person who has the skills, abilities, and behaviors to successfully connect with people in the world of work. We want that person to be you.

A connect is a person with whom you establish a mutually beneficial relationship.

We will refer to people in your network as connects, not contacts. The difference is that a contact is someone with whom you don't have a relationship, while a connect is one with whom you do. Don't worry; you may feel that you don't have much to contribute to relationships with midcareer adults and are questioning how can you create one. Well, here's what hundreds of connects have told us. Just having the privilege to assist a young person who is trying to make it is satisfaction enough. Giving the adults the satisfaction of knowing they made a difference in the life of another is enough. It's is worth the price of gold not only for your connect but for you. In essence, the receiver (you) becomes the giver. Many benefits come with the act of giving—improved self-esteem, better relationships, and increased confidence are but a few.

We have given more than three hundred presentations on helping youth connect to the world of work. Time and time again, we are astonished by the number of adults who approach us after each presentation concerned about the progress of their children. Their children may have fallen off the beaten path. They're concerned and ask us if we have any insight to share. We're talking about corporate CEOs and leaders of nonprofits.

Participating in the life of a young person is a redeeming factor for many. Some do it out of a sense of obligation, others because they want to help a young person who is trying. Some do it because of an overwhelming desire to connect with a young person when they may not have had great success connecting with their own. A large majority do it because it was done for them. They got to where they are today because of the help from someone else. Now they want to reciprocate. You have access to the greatest gift that keeps giving—caring adults. Use them, and they will work wonders for you.

When making connections, you must give something back. To sustain the connection, both parties must benefit in some way. "Givers gain" is the slogan of the world's largest networking organization, BNI. It is the belief that when people set goals to help others and honestly work to achieve these goals, they usually gain the most out of the experience—through a reciprocal benefit.

What do you have to give to the networking relationship? We'll explore this in depth during the creation of your six/seven/$uccess plan. But let's just take a quick look at a few of the ways you can serve your Connects. We call them serves.

- Refer a new customer to your connect
- Endorse your connect on social media.
- Volunteer for your connect's company/organization
- Post positive reviews on your connect's website/Facebook page
- Purchase your connect's products
- Share your expertise with your connect
- Supporting your connect's events.

Get to Work: List Seven Ways to Serve.

The greatest way to serve is by sharing the new labor-market information you received from your connect with others in your community, school, or family. You will quickly self-discover that connecting is not only about receiving, it's about giving. In this manner, you become the giver, thereby increasing your value of self and connectedness to the greater world, as many studies have demonstrated comes with the act of giving. In essence, you become the connect, and the whole process of social-capital accumulation continues and grows exponentially.

What Adults Gain

In seminars across the United States, we talk about the power of our program to educators and workforce-development professionals. They know it's important, yet rarely take active steps to teach students how to make connections or give them the support to do so. Part of the reason is policy. The problem is that we have too many 8-track schools in an MP3 world. Most schools are still doing what they did back in the early seventies. Few schools pay attention to helping students build social capital. Of the ones that do, most are Ivy-League schools. Public universities, two-year colleges, and a host of workforce-development programs haven't even broken the surface. Where it is needed most, you find it less. Little has changed despite the major changes in society, most schools are stuck on 8-track.

You don't have to be stuck on ineffective job-hunt/career-building strategies. If educators can't see the problem, it is impossible for them to fix it. You must be aware of the problem to come up with a solution. Hopefully, *MCW* will be a catalyst for change. Until then, you must make making connections a dominant part of your career-development strategy. No one will do it for you.

CONNECTING

*A great attitude does much more than turn on the
lights in our worlds; it seems to magically connect us
to all sorts of serendipitous opportunities that were
somehow absent before the change.*
~ Unknown

CONNECT WITH THE CONNECTS

F	R	F	K	O	O	B	E	C	A	F	B	A	R	L
U	E	D	A	R	S	Z	I	I	E	M	I	E	E	K
A	N	N	I	V	E	R	S	A	R	Y	R	M	T	S
L	I	A	M	E	O	R	I	L	F	Y	T	A	T	Q
Z	I	P	B	Y	P	R	I	D	N	Q	H	N	I	Y
P	K	N	L	H	E	N	I	A	A	F	D	X	W	U
S	R	I	O	V	K	S	P	T	Y	Z	A	Z	T	Y
I	S	N	E	E	E	M	T	D	E	B	Y	X	T	A
X	E	S	D	B	O	P	Q	A	L	S	B	I	I	Z
Q	U	I	E	C	G	Q	X	U	T	G	C	O	V	T
A	N	V	H	R	S	P	O	U	S	E	Q	D	H	I
S	X	D	Z	W	D	B	H	U	O	T	X	A	U	T
G	A	B	Z	I	D	D	W	E	W	K	Q	M	S	L
F	U	P	Q	U	C	V	A	W	L	G	E	R	K	E
S	L	R	I	F	H	G	J	B	Y	R	F	M	Z	Z

To effectively network, you must collect key information during the first contact. Let's have some fun. In the word puzzle, search for hidden words representing some of the key information you should obtain while connecting.

Answer Key

ADDRESS: make sure you obtain a connect's full address. Many business cards do not have addresses.

ANNIVERSARY: this will be the date your first met your connect and where.

BIRTHDAY: just day and month—you don't want to offend people by asking for the year.

CITY

COMPANY

E-MAIL

FACEBOOK: you need to ask if your connect uses social media and if it is OK for you to connect using that venue. Make sure you have prepped your rep—which you'll learn more about in chapter eight.

FAVORITES: you want to find out your connect's favorite places to visit or eat, color, music, types of books. All this information is great in helping you build relationships in the long run.

FAX: yes, people still use them.

HOBBY: it's important to ask connects what hobbies they are interested in.

LINKEDIN: LinkedIn is a great way to keep in touch with your connects and see others in their networks. You may ask for a connection to one of them at a later date.

NAME

PHONE

SPOUSE

STATE

TITLE

TWITTER

ZIP

Take some time to think about other types of information that will help you coonect.

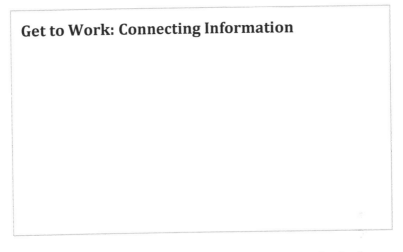

Get to Work: Connecting Information

Once you know the information you want to obtain from a connect, you need to have a plan for recording and storing it. Most connectors try to record information on a connect's business card. This approach has many difficulties. Most cards are laminated, which makes writing on them difficult unless you carry around a Sharpie (and then you'll have a smudging problem on your hand—literally). Other cards are colored or have so much text on them that there is no place to write information.

We don't recommend pulling out your phone during networking sessions. Although you are only using it to collect a connect's information, it looks too informal and disrespectful. The best bet is to carry around an MCW card or a little black book.

An MCW card is a five-by-seven index card that allows you to capture your contact's information and is easily transferable to your six/seven/$uccess spreadsheet. You can download a copy of the card at www.socialcaptialbuilders.com, or use the template below to print out your own. Print the card on card-stock paper, cut a few out, and carry them around in your wallet or purse.

Make the MCW connect cards work for you. Make notes that will help you remember how the person looks. Write down what you have in common, where they person is from, and school attended. Include details you think your connect would be pleased to know you remembered. It's an excellent way to anchor to a connect and show that you are on top of your game.

Once you have collected this information, don't let these cards sit. Within seven hours, we want you to record the information on your six/seven/$uccess spreadsheet and initiate your first touch (you will learn more about the six/seven/$uccess spreadsheet in a later chapter). It's a major problem that every connector faces because most were not taught the rules for proper follow-up.

One rule is simple. Get it done before it gets forgotten! The main reason many people don't follow up is that they wait too long and can't remember any of the specifics about the person they met. They sit there, looking at a business card with no clue about who it belongs to. All they have is a business card, and, to be honest, most can't remember when and where they got it. Cards stack, and connections slack. Hundreds of opportunities whiz by while you're sitting there hoping to find one.

Don't be scared about appearing too eager. We would rather you seem too eager than too forgetful. More than likely, your first follow-up will be something really simple, like a quick e-mail. No one will think you're a stalker because you followed up seven hours after you met. They'll think you are on-point.

Later, we'll give you ideas for different follow-ups, or touches. It's just a matter of personalizing the touch, entering the contact information, and pressing send. Each touch should take you no more than five minutes.

If you choose to make a call for your first touch, you have an 80 percent chance of getting voicemail. Once again, procrastinating about making the call makes no sense. Keep saying to yourself, "It's really not a big deal." It will help you get it done. Here is an example of a touch call: "Hello, Mr. Smith. This is Peter Black. We met at yesterday's chamber meeting. I just wanted to thank you for your recommendations. I look forward to staying in contact with you."

It's that simple.

Here are a few other points to make reaching out a little easier:

1. Watch out for noise. Don't try to connect to someone while your dog is barking, you're on a train, or while waiting in line to get into a local concert. Respect the time and quality of the short interaction. Find a quiet place where you can make calls and work uninterrupted.
2. Write down what you want to say. It's going to be less than a one-minute call. Don't stress it. Be professional and friendly.
3. Most of all, remember that if someone is going to connect, something has to move.

Not all of your connecting will take place at events. Most of your efforts will entail reaching out to family members, friends, and neighbors. All these strong-tie connections are ready to assist you. All you have to do is ask and prove you're credible. It only seems unnatural because so few people do it. Although you have seen your neighbors almost every day for the past three years, you probably don't know what they do for a living.

Connection Corner, James, Age 26

It's not about what you get; it's all about what you can give. Ironically, the more connections you can make, the more connections you're able to give. I remember taking an interest in a high school kid who worked for me. I mentored him, showed him the ropes, and introduced him to many people as I could. He took advantage of every opportunity, and he is now a manager. If I hadn't connected, I would not have been able to help him connect. I take a lot of pride in helping others, especially when I see them succeed.

Reaching out and connecting with your immediate strong ties is the brunt of our model. After you identify your connection cohort, it's time to take steps to connect. You can begin by making sure you have all of the contact information. How? Just ask!

CHAPTER EIGHT

DANGERS OF SOCIAL MEDIA

"You are what you share."
~ Charles Leadbeater

Now, before we get into the full process, let's address a few things.

Anywhere between 37 and 90 percent of companies use social media to research job candidates, and 69 percent admitted to not hiring candidates because of what appeared on their social-media pages (Mulvey, T. 2013).

Let us ask you a question, and we want another honest answer. Is your Facebook page destroying your chances for meaningful employment and connecting? Let's take a look at facts about social media and the role it can play in enhancing or destroying your connecting opportunities. Then, let's make a plan to ensure that you are not adversely affected. We call it "prep your rep."

Let's be honest; it's impossible to discuss the benefits of social media without first discussing the negatives. Corporations are using social media to vet potential employees. Yes, it will, and probably does, raise issues regarding privacy and First Amendment rights. These battles will be played out on the courtroom floor, not over your opportunity.

We have all heard social-media horror stories. No one is

immune. Corporate and government officials with access to the nation's top security systems still fall victim. Stories abound about misplaced pictures, tweets, and inappropriate posts. It seems to spread more quickly than the flu. During our program, we ask students to share social-media horror stories—times when they were totally exposed or embarrassed due to Facebook, e-mail, or texting—to reinforce the fact that you should use social media responsibly, despite the fun it brings.

Most people think that they are safe behind their privacy settings. While most legitimate social-media outlets have established privacy settings to protect the information you share and who has access to it, those settings are not infallible.

Social media is a billion-dollar industry. Money is made based on information about where people shop, what they buy, and how much they spend. Moreover, companies are looking to save millions of dollars on employee recruiting costs. An increasing number of

Connection Corner, Donald, Age 24

Some people would say I was sharp. But I guess not sharp enough.

My goal was to work for the police force. After a few months of applying, I finally got an interview. I spoke with the recruiter for several minutes about my background, experience, and training. As the interview progressed, it seemed as though things were going well, and that I had a good chance of advancing to the next stage of the process. At one point, another person came into the interview and invited me to follow him to another room. He told me to log into this computer and open up my Facebook account. They wanted to review my posts and look at the people I was connected with. I was shocked! They said if I was serious about getting the job, this would be part of the background check that I would have to be able to pass.

I wish I prepped my rep that day.

companies are turning to social media for help in finding the right candidate. Employers don't do the dirty work themselves. Due to the hidden dangers and legal implications of social-media recruitment, many companies are safeguarding their interests by using third-party vendors. These third-party vendors may use unscrupulous tactics in getting past privacy settings to uncover unsettling information about you. There are already tons of applications and algorithms working to track every one of your postings, purchases, and downloads.

For your own good, we recommend creating specific social-media accounts until the job-search process is completed. You may want to delete or suspend your other social-media accounts, at least until the job, scholarship, or raise is secured. We could spend the rest of the book showing you how to set proper privacy settings, but by the time you read the book, those suggestions will already be outdated. A major part of prepping your rep and a major responsibility of schools and programs using our process is to help students audit their social-media presence and provide support to students in keeping their online and social-media appearances safe.

There is a great YouTube clip called "Dangers of Social Networking." We use it a lot in our classes. Created by a group of high-school students, it depicts some of the things that can go wrong when you fail to prep your rep. After showing the clip to students in the program, we hear tons of laughter. When asked why they're laughing, they inform us that they know someone who has faced similar issues. Despite the preponderance of social proof that social media can hurt you, many people do not take the necessary precautions to protect their social connections.

Let's say you're a corporate CEO who meets a great young woman through a family member. She impresses you, so you give her your business card. She promptly follows up with a thank-you e-mail, and then contacts you the following week to inform you that she took action on one of your recommendations. She shares the outcomes. You are amazed and feel proud that you were able to help. You let her know that if she ever needs a recommendation, you would be glad to provide one for her.

This young woman is serious about building her social capital. She remembers that during your initial conversation, she asked you about your hobbies. You told her that you were a runner and had your first marathon coming up. Low and behold, two weeks after the marathon you get a letter in the mail. In it is a 26.2-mile sticker—the sign of a well-accomplished marathon. You say to yourself, "I like this young woman."

A week passes, and she calls you, but you're busy. Your assistant takes the call. She informs your assistant that she is applying for a job at another firm and would like your recommendation. Your assistant writes down the message but decides to do her own vetting. She looks up the young woman on Facebook and sends a friend request. The young woman quickly accepts her request, because that's what she does—accepts everyone's request. Your assistant discovers tons of half-nude pictures of the young woman with her sorority sisters partying hard during spring break. She gets back to you and recommends that you rethink giving the young woman your recommendation.

This is just one example. There are many. However, on the opposite side of the spectrum, some managers have stated that social media can have a positive impact on a potential employee.

A survey from Career Builder reports that hiring managers found that the following information contained in an applicant's social-media pages positively influenced their hiring decisions:

- evidence of a good personality
- professional image
- background information
- range of interests
- communication skills
- creativity
- references

Conversely, hiring managers stated that the following items were reasons not to hire a candidate:

- provocative/inappropriate photos/info
- drinking or using drugs
- poor communication skills
- bad-mouthing of previous employer
- discriminatory comments related to race, gender, religion, and so on
- lied about qualifications

The strategy is to make sure your social media works for you. So what if you have to take down a site or two. Your friends will understand when they see you with a job or scholarship.

It's time for you to use the social-media checklist to audit your social-media pages. Make copies of the page, and use one for every social-media outlet you use.

Social Media Outlet:		Date:
Postings	Items	None—------------Many *1 2 3 4 5 6 7 8*
Provocative or inappropriate photos	0	1 2 3 4 5 6 7 8
Provocative or inappropriate info	0	1 2 3 4 5 6 7 8
Evidence of drinking or drug use	0	1 2 3 4 5 6 7 8
Demonstration of poor communication skills	8	1 2 3 4 5 6 7 8
Evidence of discriminatory comments related to race, gender, religion, etc.	0	1 2 3 4 5 6 7 8
Extreme political/social postings	0	1 2 3 4 5 6 7 8
Evidence of physical or mental-health issues	0	1 2 3 4 5 6 7 8
	Total Score	

Rating Scale
8—16:   Make adjustments
17–48:   Replace social-media outlets with more appropriate ones
49+   Get off social media

Before we go further, we need you to prep your rep, and do it often. Let us ask you, what will you gain by doing so? Would you be willing to spend thirty minutes a week prepping your rep? What would you gain?

We are not saying that all social media is bad. It really is up to you. However, just to be safe, you should take active steps to prep your rep. It might be a good idea to ask a connect to evaluate your social-media presence using the social-media evaluation sheet. In that way, you can show that person the effort you're making to connect. Also, you will be passing along an important resource to share with his or her kids. Your connect will love you for it.

Chapter Eight

TOUCH TRUMPS TECHNOLOGY ALL THE TIME

"Appreciation wins out over self-promotion every time."
~ Kody Bateman

Don't get social media confused with connecting. It's not. While some social-media sites claim to be the twenty-first century version of the dinner table, they're far from it. Given its negative impact on young people's future economic opportunity, we feel it hurts more than it helps.

We have a saying: "Touch trumps technology all the time!" We understand that personally connecting with your connects may not always be possible. People are busy. Nevertheless, making the extra effort is worth it. A face-to-face meeting is the most powerful method for connecting. Make sure you use it. When we talk about personally connecting, we aren't talking about schmoozing at a social-networking mixer; we're emphasizing lunch at a quiet local restaurant, meeting for a cup of coffee, or having a sandwich in the park. Breaking bread with others is a great way to get them in your corner.

At Social Capital Builders, we urge our partner sites to develop social-capital-building opportunities for students. We make it a rule to take capital collectors to at least 30 percent of the professional events we attend. We ask them to join us at business dinners, receptions, and events. If schools believe that making connections is the pathway to future success, then why wouldn't they make this type of commitment? It just

Connection Corner, Martin, Age 18

I was a H.S. junior who wasn't much interested in school. It was too easy and, honestly, not that important, at least to me. All I wanted to do was play around with technology. I knew I had to connect to something or I would drop-out of school.

I volunteered at a local tech program that helped underprivileged kids learn STEM careers. I wasn't as much interested in helping them as much as helping myself. I knew that group would be meeting a lot of key people in the tech field, and I wanted to be right there with them whenever I could. I grew to love working with the kids and helping them learn to code and build computers. I forgot about my purpose and started to focus on helping others.

I chaperoned the group to a major tech retailer, where I made direct contact with the manager. He asked me if I wanted a job.

requires training in the process, and then we let them fly. All we have to do is serve as their wingpeople.

Here are some examples of professional events we attend:

Conferences
Workshops
Webinars
Board meetings
Fundraising presentations
Speeches
Breakfast business meetings
Business luncheons
Job fairs

Many young people who attend these events find out about jobs, scholarships, and other forms of assistance. It works and has been working for years. Why schools and workforce programs don't make this a strategic part of the curriculum lies beyond us.

Countless Ivy-League schools organize connecting events for seniors and late-year juniors. Program alumni are invited in for an evening where they can interact with current students. Connecting may be taken seriously at Ivy-League institutions and private schools; however, the same zeal is not present when it comes to public institutions and programs. It is time for everyone to wake up to the need for this service. And it's time for you to take responsibility for building your social capital because no one is going to do it or you.

You need resources to connect. You don't need a lot, just some. Similar to the need to invest in a business suit or a nice pair of shoes before an interview, you need to invest in social-capital-building tools. You need a connecting budget. We know—college life is rough. That's why you bought this book. We're giving it to you real. If you save $10 a week, by the end of the year, you will have saved $520 for social-capital building. With an average price of lunch at $20, you can take each of the 24 people in your cohort out to lunch. The truth is, If you get them to go, there is an 80 percent chance that they will refuse to let you pay.

On holidays, ask parents and relatives for restaurant gift cards, memberships to networking associations, subscriptions to contact-management systems, automated card-sending programs, or registration for a premium LinkedIn account. Most of these programs cost less than one hundred dollars— much less than a brand new pair of designer jeans. Once armed with a solid contact-management/e-mail system, card-sending program, and other resources for connecting, you will be an unstoppable collector.

(Special note: If you are under eighteen years of age, you need to have your parents' consent and supervision when reaching out to adults.)

Here is a list of some of our favorite networking tools that you should ask parents and relatives to help you obtain:

- Starbucks gift cards (or the coffee shop of your choice)
- restaurant gift cards
- SendOutCards.com

- LinkedIn premium membership
- contact-management software with autoresponder program (iContact, Constant Contact, etc.)
- chamber of commerce membership (you may have to registrar as a sole proprietor)
- membership in professional trade associations, depending on your interests
- Rotaract Clubs (junior version of Rotary Clubs)
- alumni associations
- business cards
- professional voicemail
- website

Connecting Opportunities

These are everywhere. You don't have to go to a formal networking mixer. You can make connections to anyone, at any time, in anyplace—as long as you are prepared. The point of networking is to network. It is not "sitwork" or "lookwork." Don't use the Starbucks drive-through; go into the restaurant. Don't use the automated checkout counter; wait in line. Don't pick up your movie ticket from the ticketing machine; wait in line for the box office. Learn how to strike up conversations. Often a simple hi and a quick follow-up question will do.

Here are a few examples:

Coffee Shop
"Hi. My name's Joe. It's feeling like a mocha chocolate-chip latte day for me, how about you?"

Supermarket
"A lot of people don't use those automated checkout counters. I'm one of them. What's your reason?"

Movies
"Must be a good movie. What have you heard?"

Then follow up with a conversation starter question:
"So what do you do?"
"I just graduated from high school/college. Any recommendations?"
"You look like you've got it together. What's your secret?"

Connecting opportunities are all around you. Open your eyes to the plethora of ways to connect and build with others. Don't take the quick route. Take time and make the connection, flash a smile, make eye contact. Do it, and keep on doing it. Do it until a connection is made, a conversation started, a relationship blooms.

It is imperative that you identify connecting opportunities in your city/region. In our program, we have wingpersons who work with students in identifying at least twenty connecting opportunities in their local area.

Opportunities are all around you. We continue to be amazed by the number of students who can't come up with a list of ten. Most struggle to list five. It's because few people recognize the impact of connecting and its importance in the job hunt/career search.

We have found it necessary to help jar students' minds regarding the possible range of opportunities. Here is a list of connection event joggers that will help you identify opportunities:

- What meetup.com groups can you join?
- What chamber association is in your area, and where does it meet?
- Where and when do city planning commission meetings take place?
- What reunions are coming up?
- Ever thought about guest speaking at your former grade, middle, and high schools?

- Who is holding a fundraiser?
- What events need volunteers?
- Where are 90 percent of the political rallies/demonstrations held?
- Ever go to church, synagogue, or mosque?
- What are the local sporting activities and competitions, and have you joined?
- Are you a member of a local fitness club?

Put together a list of at least twelve events that you will attend over the next three months. Record the time, date, and location, and the strategy you will use to meet at least three people at each meeting. For example:

Place: Council Member Renee Smith's Community Meeting Date: June 30, 20xx Location: Fisher Community Center	Strategy: Meet with council member's staff before event. Let them know about my job search. Inform them I am coming to the meeting and would appreciate if they could direct me to key people who they think can help.

My Connection Events

(List 12 local events that you will use for Social-Capital-Building).

Place: Date: Location:	Strategy:

The possibilities are endless. It just takes a little effort, and you will set your job hunt on fire. In each city, there are tons of business meetings, conferences, seminars, networking events, and trainings. It is your job to get to these events. The best way to get there is to use your initial connects to help you blaze the trail.

Not only will you be able to make connections, but you will have the opportunity to practice the skills learned in this book. The more events you attend, the more connects you engage. The more connects you engage, the better your chances for a well-paying job and a satisfying career.

It may be as simple as visiting a website, researching dates, and then showing up. You'll be amazed how quickly your cohort will develop and the opportunities you'll receive. But it's our bet that you won't have to do much outside connecting because you already know the people who will get you your next job. The challenge is to act like it.

SIX/SEVEN/$UCCESS

"Nothing happens till someone connects."
~Edward DeJesus

Are you ready to make connections work? It's time we got down to the cold, hard plan. This plan was created after twenty-plus years observing what makes young adults successful in the world of work, and three years of intense research and interviews with over one hundred workforce experts, employers, and gainfully employed young adults. We are confident in our recommendations, and we hope that you place as much effort into the process as you do in traditional job-hunt strategies.

Over the next few pages, you will focus on developing a six/seven/$uccess plan and learn the skills necessary to implement the plan. Six/seven/$uccess is a surefire way to build and sustain labor-market connections and, ultimately, economic self-sufficiency. It will require an investment of at least thirty-six minutes a day for a return of a lifetime of future economic opportunity.

Six/seven/$uccess stands for six connects and seven contacts each for long-term success.

The first step in the six/seven/$uccess plan is to learn anchoring skills. Anchoring is the process of getting a person emotionally invested in helping you achieve your FEO goals. Without a good anchoring technique, our program will be difficult. As a young adult, you may feel that you don't have much to offer. This isn't true. You are offering someone the opportunity to help, to make a difference.

People are looking for opportunities to help young adults who are trying to help themselves. You hear daily, "Today's young people don't want to work for anything..." Adults are searching for that one young person who can prove them wrong. Let that person be you.

In our research, we have found that it's best for young adults to have a clear, memorable script—we call this the YOUTRY statement. It should meet five standards:

- introduce the young adult
- identify the young adult's goals
- define why the young adult wants to attain these goals
- asks for advice on those goals
- asks for a connect's follow-up contact information

Anchoring Through YOUTRY Statements

As we move on in the process, we will introduce add-ons to the YOUTRY statement that will increase its effectiveness. After you obtain a certain degree of comfort, you may abandon your YOUTRY format to seek out a style that is natural to you. However, our experience has taught us that a well-trained capital collector is better than an untrained one. Knowing what you are going to say and how you are going to say it will take tons of stress off your back and put you at ease in your connection relationships.

The first step in anchoring is making sure that you know your immediate goals and can articulate them to others. It is the first part of your YOUTRY statement. Connectors often don't know what they want to get out of the networking relationship. To make a connection, you need to know what you want. You don't want to waste someone's time by being unclear, and you don't want people to try to figure out how they can help.

Think of it like dating. How long will your partner stay with you if you don't know what you want? Probably not long. If your partner has any sense, he or she will ask you your intentions from the beginning. Most connects have full lives and will appreciate your directness.

We advise you to make your goals FEO focused. Remember that FEO focused means:

- Skills: What workforce skills are you trying to learn and master? (i.e., use of Excel, business writing, project management, public speaking, equipment operations, etc.)
- Degrees: What undergraduate or graduate degree are you seeking, and why?
- Work Experience: What type of work experience will help you advance in the world of work? What do you need to get out of that work experience?
- Positive adult connections: Who do you want to know and why? How can they contribute to your future career success?
- Credentials: What credentials can lead you to well-paying jobs?

Your FEO goals should be measurable and realistic and ones that people can help you achieve. Here are some examples:

- learn fundraising skills
- complete my college education
- obtain employment in the health-care industry
- connect with an executive in the health-care industry
- learn more about six-sigma certification

Depending on your career interest and level of academic attainment, your goal statements may change. In fact, we are sure of it. Changing goals are fine. Not having someone to help you achieve them isn't.

LIST FIVE FEO GOALS:

I'm trying to…
(Skill)

I'm trying to…
(Work
experience)

I'm trying to…
(Credential)

I'm trying to…
(Networks)

I'm trying to…
(Degrees)

The second part of anchoring involves knowing *why* you are seeking that particular goal.

The "why" is a heartfelt statement about your goal, the reason you are actually going through your program. It has to be something really big and really meaningful, something that will make connects and others who hear it feel thrilled and excited each time you recite it. It's something you want so badly it keeps you up at night. It gives you a worthy reason to get up in the morning. Some call it a "vision statement." We call it YOUTRY.

Connects like hearing a *why* statement because it lets them know you're motivated and have a reason to reach your goal. They like it when people refuse to be labeled victims who are just reacting to circumstances. Having a *why* statement shows that you are in control. Connects have every reason to believe that the effort they put into you will pay off. Not for them—it

Connection Corner, Carlos, Age 38

I met Rasheed at a fundraising dinner for a local Goodwill agency. He was one of 10 at-risk kids the agency had brought in to talk to us about the impact the program has had on their lives. Most of the stories were the same; however, Rasheed's was a little different.

He talked about how he liked to box and that it helped give him a little more discipline, which made competing in the program a little easier. I used to box as an amateur and wanted to share this fact with this young man. I approached him and introduced myself. He was so nervous but extremely kind. We talked about boxing and our lofty goals of one day making it to the pros. In fact, we had both fought at the same weight class.

I told Rasheed that I work out at a local boxing gym, and he would be welcome to come. The following week, I got a call from Rasheed, and he joined me for a few training sessions. We spent more time talking than training. I grew close to him. I haven't seen him in a few months though. Rasheed always wanted to go off to college. A few friends at my law firm helped me make sure that happened. Rasheed is now in his junior year at Community College, and he is doing well. Boxing is not in his future, but a college degree sure is.

I am so glad my wife made me go to that event. I found a young man who needed me probably as much as I needed him. He will be a friend for life.

will pay off for you.

Everyone wants to be down with a winner.

Sample Why Statements:

My Name is Mark Jones. I am in my second year at Lincoln Community College. I want to graduate from the program and go to a four-year college to get a degree in psychology. I am trying because I want to help young adults, like myself, who have been abandoned by the people who said they love them. I want to show them that there are people who care if they are given the chance. FEO focus area: degrees.

My Name is Alicia Smith. I am a participant at the Youth Opportunity Center. I am trying to get into a construction apprenticeship position. I am trying because I want to show other young women that they can be successful in nontraditional careers for women. FEO focus area: experience.

My Name is Rashid Avery. I am a high-school senior. I am trying to get a driver's license. I am trying because I want to take advantage of the good employment opportunities outside of my neighborhood so I can afford to help pay for my college education. FEO focus area: credential.

Now it's your turn. Complete your Why statement. Keep in mind that they must be written in a way that will get adults personally and emotionally invested in your goals.

List One Reason You Want to Accomplish the Above Goals

I'm trying to...
because...

I'm trying to...
because...

I'm trying to...
because...

I'm trying to...
because...

I'm trying to...
because...

Let's put it all together in a way that will help you build a solid statement. Complete one YOUTRY statement for each goal.

Statement A

1. My name is

   _____.

2. I'm a student at

   _____.

3. I'm trying to

   _____.

4. I'm trying because

   _____.

5. If I may ask, what recommendations might you have for someone like me who is trying to make it?

6. That's very helpful! May I have your contact information so I can stay in contact with you for further advice and to update you on my progress?

Statement B

1. My name is

   _____.

2. I'm a student at

   _____.

3. I'm trying to

   _____.

4. I'm trying because

   _____.

5. If I may ask, what recommendations might you have for someone like me who is trying to make it?

6. That's very helpful! May I have your contact information so I can stay in contact with you for further advice and to update you on my progress?

Statement C

1. My name is

   _____.

2. I'm a student at

   _____.

3. I'm trying to

   _____.

4. I'm trying because

   _____.

5. If I may ask, what recommendations might you have for someone like me who is trying to make it?

6. That's very helpful! May I have your contact information so I can stay in contact with you for further advice and to update you on my progress?

Statement D

1. My name is

   _____.

2. I'm a student at

   _____.

3. I'm trying to

   _____.

4. I'm trying because

   _____.

5. If I may ask, what recommendations might you have for someone like me who is trying to make it?

6. That's very helpful! May I have your contact information so I can stay in contact with you for further advice and to update you on my progress?

Statement E

1. My name is

    _____.

2. I'm a student at

    _____.

3. I'm trying to

    _____.

4. I'm trying because

    _____.

5. If I may ask, what recommendations might you have for someone like me who is trying to make it?

6. That's very helpful! May I have your contact information so I can stay in contact with you for further advice and to update you on my progress?

Now let's practice. Find your wingperson. If you don't have one, a relative or friend will do. You may be able to get a connect to help you practice.

Face each other. Hand your YOUTRY statements to the other person. That person should call out the corresponding letter for a particular YOUTRY statement. When the letter is called out, you have one minute to recite your entire YOUTRY statement to your partner. If the YOUTRY statement is recited perfectly, your partner crosses it off the list and then calls out the next letter.

Connects are busy people. Their window of attention usually closes after fifteen seconds. In order to capture their attention, you must capitalize on the effectiveness of your YOUTRY statements. They need to be works of art—compelling, convincing, and captivating.

Please visit www.socialcaptialbuilders.com for some other samples of moving YOUTRY statements.

The Plan

During the rest of this chapter, we get into the core of the six/seven/$uccess plan. The foundation of the plan is your initial six connects.

We developed the six/seven/$uccess plan because we got tired of seeing large numbers of students graduating from community colleges, four-year colleges, and even from job-training programs, only to wind up unemployed. Moreover, we found many college graduates underemployed—holding jobs that don't require their education, experience, or training. Don't let that be you.

53 percent of America's recent college graduates are either unemployed or working in jobs that don't require a college diploma (Associated Press, 2012). That's ridiculous. In our seminars, we state, "Well-paying jobs are out there; you just can't find them." So much of the youth-unemployment dilemma stems from the fact that youth are not trained in how to properly connect or supported in properly doing so.

Most schools and workforce programs don't have a strategy to help youth develop the skills, tools, and support to build social capital. Neither do most parents. They simply aren't paying attention to the number-one way people find jobs—connecting.

Now that you're ready with your YOUTRY statement, it's time to start the process.

The six/seven/$uccess model equals six connects/seven points of contact/for Success (or as we like to say, the building of FEO (skills, credentials, work experience, degrees, and positive employment networks.)

It should be done as follows.

1. Collect Contacts.
    In the first session, you identified strong ties and weak ties. Now is the time to put those contacts to use. In addition, on a daily basis, apply the anchoring techniques you learned earlier in this chapter to add contacts to your list. Review the six/seven/$uccess form.

    For at least twenty-four contacts (they become connects once you start the six/seven/$uccess process with them), you should have prepared the following information. If you haven't, stop, go back, and get it.

    Name:
    Company:
    Title:
    Full address:
    Phone:
    E-mail:
    Place of employment:
    Birthday:
    Connection points:

2. Develop a list of touches (Ts).
    A touch is any way you can reach out and stay in contact with someone.

3. Develop a list of serves (Ss).
    A serve is anything you can do to assist one of your connects with personal or professional goals.

4. Develop a list of Requests (Rs).
    A request is something that your connect can do to help you develop your FEO.

Procedure

Actively work on connecting with six connects each week for a total of seven weeks. This will complete one cycle. Four cycles equals twenty-four contacts, which equals a cohort.

The six/seven/$uccess form is based on one cycle. During the first week, you will initiate a touch with each of the six connects. In the second week, you will initiate another touch with the same six connects. During the third week, you will perform a serve. In the fourth week, you issue a specific FEO request, followed by two more touches and another request. At the end of the seven weeks, the cycle is completed, and you evaluate the efficacy of each connect using the rating system.

Once a connect has completed the six/seven/$uccess cycle, the connect should be entered into a quarterly e-mail update program. Extremely active connects can be carried on to the next cohort, and continue the process as before. Then add more connects to your list to begin cycle two, and proceed as before.

The full cohort should be exhausted after twenty-eight weeks. At that time, you should see some serious gains in your FEO and career objectives, and you will have twenty-seven people who are fully engaged in helping you build your FEO.

Touches/Serves/Requests

A "touch" is any way you can reach out and stay in contact with someone. List the ways you can "touch" a connect. For example, a phone call, card, or letter. The most touches one of our groups ever came up with was twenty-one. Push the limit.

It is imperative that you have a touch method that you are comfortable with. More importantly, it should be one that you are prepared to deliver at a moment's notice. For example, an e-mail follow-up is a touch. So is a thank-you card. More advanced touches include personal video messages, a Facebook compliment, and so on. We don't want you to tailor touches at this point. That's something you can do later, after you are comfortable with the six/seven/$uccess process.

Now take the time to perfect your message. Check spelling, secure software, buy the cards, and open up an account. These items are your lifeline to your connects. Secure them now. Don't put too much effort into what should be a simple process. On the next page, brainstorm all the possible ways you can realistically touch a connect.

WAYS TO TOUCH A CONNECT...

Serving is the most important and, by far, the simplest, part of the six/seven/$uccess process. Most adults know you don't have a nickel in your pocket. They won't expect a gift or tickets to Wimbledon. What they want to see is evidence that you're serious about your future and genuinely appreciative of their help.

When serving, keep it simple. Think of something easy, not way outside of your comfort zone. Referring someone to your connect is one example. Find someone—a new customer, another professional in the same industry, a person or group who can help grow the business—and then connect them.

Other examples include:

- volunteering at or helping raise funds for their favorite charity
- helping your connect with an unfinished project
- sending articles related to their interests
- painting a room

All are good examples. A little serve goes a long way. A serve is anything you can do to assist one of your connects with personal or professional goals.

OK, your turn. List possible ways to serve your connects. The record for listing serves was fifteen. Let's see if you can do better.

WAYS TO SERVE A CONNECT...

The request is hardest part of the process in general, and the six/seven/$uccess plan in particular. People don't like to ask for help, especially young adults. Some consider it a sign of weakness or desperation when, in fact, it is a sign of emotional maturity and intelligence.

A request is something that your connect can do to help you develop your FEO goals. You must push yourself to make requests. Remember; requests should only come after two touches and one serve. At that point, most connects will be more than willing to extend a helping hand. Here are some samples of requests. On the next page, make a list of your own.

I need help getting my driver's license.
I need help finding work experience.
I need a letter of reference.
I need help paying college application fees.

WHAT TO REQUEST FROM A CONNECT...

It's OK if connects say no. Some will; some won't. So what? Someone's waiting.

Throughout the six/seven/$uccess plan, you will have the opportunity to gain key workforce opportunities and knowledge through your active network. It's your job to make sure they take action and follow the plan.

Measuring Your Success
Actively work on the six/seven/$uccess process for at least twenty-six minutes a day. During that time, you will issue touches, serves, and requests. You will also work on identifying strong ties, corresponding weak ties, and make plans to turn them into connects through the delivery of your YOUTRY statement. You will identify and attend connecting events when needed and only with a wingperson to keep the flow of connects coming and to expand your circle of influence.

Sounds like a lot? It's really simple once you get the hang of it. But there is one more part, the evaluation. What gets measured gets done! We don't want you to waste your time or

Connection Corner, Raphael, Age 18

The payoff is huge! I'm always on social media, and I make it my business to hit up theparents of my friends. It has made getting a job a snap.

I start to break the ice by just liking something they post on Facebook or responding to a comment they made on Twitter. Of course, it's always something positive.

My aunt was raising money for a non-profit, and I logged on and told her how proud I was of her. Like,five of her friends sent me friend requests. I grew connections in less than a minute. One of her friends told me about a scholarship her company was offering. I got a job and the quickest $500 I have ever earned.

your connects'. The FEO outcomes assessment helps you maximize your gains by tracking your connects' impact on each of your five FEO areas.

Let's review. There are seven interactions in our process. Five of the interactions are about nothing more than building a connection and solidifying a relationship. Only two of the seven interactions entail making a request for a specific FEO or career goal.

The FEO outcomes assessment will help you measure your connect's impact in each area. We are not saying that you should make gains in each area (we hope you do); it serves as a guide to help you focus on making sure you get something tangible out of the connection. We want you to use this data for the monitoring of the efficacy of the process, your motivation, and to ensure your fidelity to the six/seven/$uccess formula.

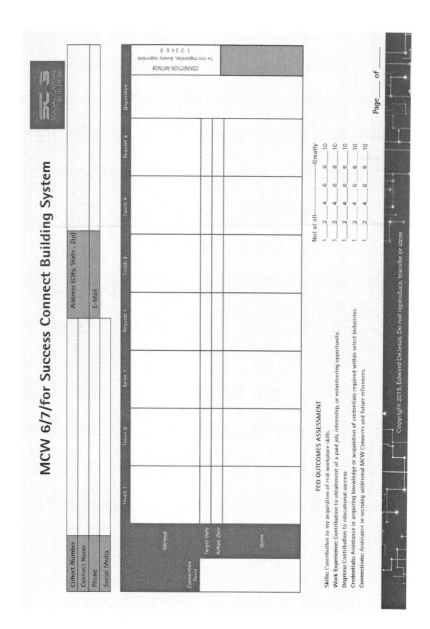

MCW 6/7/for Success Connect Building System

Cohort Number		Address (City, State , Zip)
Connect Name		
Phone		E-Mail
Social Media		

	Touch 1	Touch 2	Serve 1	Request 1	Touch 3	Touch 4	Request 2	Disposition
Method								
Target Date								
Actual Date								
Connection Point								
Notes								

CONNECTION RATING#

1= non responsive, 6=very responsive
1 2 3 4 5 6

FEO OUTCOMES ASSESSMENT

Skills: Contribution to my acquisition of real workplace skills.

Work Experience: Contribution to obtainment of a paid job, internship, or volunteering opportunity.

Degrees: Contribution to educational success

Credentials: Assistance in acquiring knowledge or acquisition of credentials required within select industries

Connections: Assistance in securing additional MCW Connects and future references.

Not at all------------------Greatly
1 _2_ _4_ _6_ _8_ _10
1 _2_ _4_ _6_ _8_ _10
1 _2_ _4_ _6_ _8_ _10
1 _2_ _4_ _6_ _8_ _10
1 _2_ _4_ _6_ _8_ _10

Page____ of____

Beyond helping you secure a job, the system should help you gain the five elements of FEO that are instrumental to your future success.

1. Work experience

The acquisition of early work experience is the key to your future economic success. According to research conducted by Dr. Andy Sum, the director of the Center for Labor Market Studies at Northeastern University, early work experience strongly improves young workers' prospects for future success in the job market. You should use your connects to help you gain the following from a variety of work-experience opportunities:

1. Uncover the myriad of work-experience opportunities available (internships, job shadowing, externships, volunteer, paid, full-time, part-time, seasonal, temporary).
2. Gain a documented history of attendance and punctuality.
3. Secure the references of work-experience supervisors.
4. Make connections with other gainfully employed people.
5. Gain key labor-market information and analysis from people at the source.

2. Skills

A skill is the learned capacity to carry out predetermined results, often with a minimum outlay of time, energy, or both. The majority of skill building does not need to take place in a classroom. Each day you are afforded the opportunity to develop a host of skills that could ultimately lead to your long-term self-sufficiency, if only you are guided and supported in doing so.

The greatest source of information about the skills necessary for labor-market success comes from your connects. Information received from a closely held group of friends and associates is more impactful and relevant than any other source of labor-market information. Unfortunately, many poorly connected young people do not have people in their lives who can provide them with this important resource. That's not you, Capital Collector!

Our goal is to make sure you utilize the power of connecting to gain critical information about the skills needed for future labor-market success. It is imperative to structure networking opportunities in a way that helps you understand:

- the value of skills already possessed
- skills relevant to success in that industry
- methods of acquiring those skills
- how to translate those skills into economic opportunity

3. Positive Supportive Adult Connections

The employment success of youth is tied to the employment success of adults. It is all interrelated. If you lived in a poor community, then by definition, the majority of people in that community are either unemployed or underemployed. Building connections with a lot of unemployed people will keep you unemployed. If everyone has the same labor-market information, the information becomes stagnant, and so do people's lives. However, if you live around many employed people, then different labor-market information is shared. Information about who is hiring, who is getting fired, new company projects, needed skills, and so on opens up, and opportunity does with it.

In our process we assist you in:

1. identifying supportive adults to assist you with future opportunity connections
2. establishing plans to continue development and utilization of supportive adult connections

4. Credentials

The US Department of Labor's Bureau of Labor Statistics (BLS) reports that there will be a limited surge in the need for college-educated workers over the next decade. However, there will be a need for individuals with postsecondary education credentials for high-paying jobs. Despite this fact, credentials are the least understood and most often overlooked postsecondary educational option.

In our process, we assist you with:

1. identification of availability, costs, and benefits of credentials in your local area and
2. opportunities to obtain credentials.

5. Degrees

Your completion of high-school and postsecondary education has a direct impact on your future economic opportunity. Yet more students drop out of the postsecondary educational system than those who complete it—65 percent of community-college and 58 percent of four-year-college students don't complete the requirements for graduation within four years (U.S. Dept. of Education, 2016).

Given the lack of affordability of postsecondary education, limited basic skills, and lack of career information, many students are looking past these opportunities and get stuck in the low-wage labor market.

Your connects can be great sources of assistance and

inspiration when it comes to achieving postsecondary educational success, helping you by:

1. mentoring you and providing you with motivational support
2. helping put your education in career context
3. assisting with securing resources to continue or pay for school
4. advising you on career pathways and educational programs

At the end of the six/seven/$uccess management tool, you will see a numerical rating box pertaining to each of the five areas of FEO. Rate each connect's contribution to your development in each area.

CHAPTER ELEVEN

CONNECTION POINTS

"You can make more friends in two months by becoming interested in other people than you can in two years by trying to get other people interested in you."

~ Dale Carnegie

Connection Corner, Kevin, Age 21

I was first introduced to Mr. Martin in the 7th grade. I chose to take his computer science class instead of band,as I had the year before. I loved learning about computers and soon proved to be one of Mr. Martin's best pupils. I came to class early and helped Mr. Martin set up new terminals before school started. Eventually, Mr. Martin trusted me enough to send me on errands to help other teachers in the school who were having computer problems. Two years later, when Mr. Martin started a computer training company, he hired me to work as an assistant. Even though I was only in high school, I found my first job by being helpful to a teacher.

Your success in getting connects to act on your behalf depends on the effort you place in getting them anchored to your goals. Stated simply, it's about getting them to like you. To achieve this, you need to know your goals, be able to express them, and demonstrate, each and every week, the measurable actions you are taking to achieve them. Connections are like muscles—the more you work them, the stronger they become. Let's get strong!

Making connections is easier than you think. It just requires that you take the time to find connection points. Connection points are interests, activities, and background information you can use to build meaningful relationships. Both you and your connect may have run cross-country track in high school or served on a school newspaper. That's a connection point. Have you ever seen two people connect over being raised in the same location? They act like they are best of friends, although they never actually met before. In this world of high-speed Internet access, we so desperately want to connect to our fellow human beings over something more than a computer screen.

While there are a few adults who don't care to work with youth, most do. The late Peter Benson, former CEO of the Search Institute, said that a positive, caring adult was one of the biggest factors in the success of a young adult. We concur. The problem is that most adults don't know how to help. There has been little discourse among policy makers and people at your dinner table about how to do this and do it well.

- How often have your parents arranged career-specific lunches between you and one of their professional colleagues?
- How does your school help you build and sustain connections?
- What tools does your family provide to help you make and sustain connections?

Parents get excited about attending their younger child's soccer game but often overlook the potential of connecting you with the parents of their teammates. Have you ever considered the value (social capital) of all those employed parents? Do you think any one of them could help you find a job? Unfortunately, most of these opportunities are missed.

Finding should not be your problem. If a connect's child is part of a team, going to support him or her is a good way to anchor. Finding out the team's schedule and sending the kid good-luck notes before a game is a way to blow the connect out of the water and build a lifetime relationship. You may say you don't have the time to do these things, but we say you do! Most people would jump at spending ten minutes filling out an online job application. Many will spend up to two hours looking for work and filling out applications online. How long does it take to send someone a card or an encouraging letter about an upcoming event? Not much. Both are examples of connection points and how they are used to build meaningful relationships. Get to it.

We want you to think about how people in your community show a sense of connection. For example:

...play sports together
...use nicknames
...common sport teams

What are some of the ways you see connections play out in your community? Activities, sports, hobbies, and common experiences are all connection points and major factors that bring people together.

OK, it's time now to figure out your connection points. Connection points are the keys to helping you build strong connections. You will be amazed by how much you have in common with others. Build off these connections, and yield positive results for yourself and your family.

You can use connection points as catalysts for building long-term, mutually beneficial relationships. Let's take a look at some connection questions, and then you can work on developing your own:

- What activities do you participate in during your free time?
- What hobbies do you enjoy to help relieve stress?

- What are some of the best books you have read about success?
- Where do you like to go to unwind?

We will give you the opportunity to integrate connection questions into your YOUTRY statements. They are a surefire way to secure the information you need to build good connections.

We want you to think about the people on your strong-tie list. Is there anyone who stands out? Go ahead and write them down. For example, if a connect enjoys antique autos, you can use this information to invite him or her to an auto show or send a flyer about an upcoming one. There are probably many other connection points, but right now you just want one or two per connect so that you can start the process.

Identify how you can find out about your connects' interests, and develop one connection strategy to use with each person.

Connect	Connection Points	How could you use this information?
Kimberly Michaels	Has my dream car.	I could speak to her about how she likes the car and offer to help her maintain it.
Brian Adamas	We both love small dogs. Has a shih tzu named Bingo.	I could offer to walk the dog when he is away on business or vacations.

Now it's time to incorporate connection points into your YOUTRY statement. Make sure you get this information at the initial meeting so you can use it throughout your six/seven/$ process.

YOUTRY Plus Connection

Hi, Mr. Jones. My name is Rashid Smith. I just graduated from Fresno State University. I am looking for a full-time position in the field of juvenile justice. I am trying because I want to help young people get a fair chance at life, even if they weren't given the support and guidance I received growing up. I want to help them build opportunities and overcome issues. I want to see if you had a minute to tell me what you had to do to be successful.

Add Connecting Question

Where did you grow up, and what activities kept you busy and out of trouble?
What are some of the best books you have read on success?
Who are your role models, and why?

I enjoyed speaking with you and getting your perspective. Would you be willing to provide your contact information so that I may keep you updated on my progress?

Write out your
YOUTRY STATEMENT,
and add in at least three
connection-point questions.

Make this modification to your YOUTRY statement, and you are almost a capital collector. You have the skills, talents, and abilities to build a strong future.

THE MCW MINDSET AND ASSESSMENT

"Success is a mindset; not a location."
~ Keith Hosea

You must control undermining mind-sets. These will derail your connecting efforts quicker than a bad drug habit will. Here are some examples:

1. being uncomfortable
2. fear of rejection
3. frustration with people who don't respond
4. not knowing what to do
5. lacking patience for relationships to develop
6. understanding how to use networking tools and resources

Being comfortable with being uncomfortable is the first place to start. This is a normal part of the process when making connections and building social capital. Sometimes you may feel overwhelmed, or fear the possibility of rejection. All you need to do is speak to your wingperson. There isn't one successful person who has not faced these feelings. It's what you do about them that makes the difference. Let's take a look at what you can do to alleviate some of these mind-sets.

1. Uncomfortable, especially with people you don't know

In our process, you should never initially connect alone. At all connecting opportunities, you should have a wingperson with you. In our model, the wingperson is another capital collector or an MCW facilitator. If you are not part of an MCW chapter, then you want to find one. Visit socialcapitalbuilders.com for a listing of chapters near you. You and your wingperson can attack the opportunity together, create a friendly competition, and hold each other accountable for follow-up. Follow-up Fridays can be when you review your plan and make sure all essential contacts for that week have been made. Each Friday, set aside at least thirty-six minutes to work on all follow-up activity.

2. Fear of rejection

Contact the opportunity organizers in advance and let them know about your hesitations and fears. They may share the list of attendees so you can research who is attending, their companies/industries, and personal interests. Just ask the organizers for introductions. They will be happy to help. In fact, it's part of their job.

3. Frustration with people who don't respond

Not all people will respond to your connection efforts. This doesn't mean they are bad people; it might mean they're too busy, or that, for whatever reason, they don't feel the impetus to connect with you. It happens. They may meet another young adult the next day, and a connection is made. Perhaps the connection point is stronger. Maybe the young adult's strong tie has a greater influence. Whatever the reason, you cannot be disappointed with people who don't respond. Just be courteous, and move on.

4. Don't know what to do

I don't think so. At every event, your goal is to connect with three people. We define a satisfactory connection as the delivery of your YOUTRY statement, learning something about the potential connect, and obtaining all pertinent contact information. Your six/seven/$uccess plan is clearly laid out with the work you must do. Use your wingperson to hold you accountable.

5. Lacking patience for relationships to develop

Are you an impatient person? Do you want things to happen now and get upset when they don't? Making and building connections takes time. You should invest in this process now, not when you need it. Relationships will take weeks to develop. In the six/seven/$uccess process, you can go at least four weeks before you issue a request to someone to help you develop your FEO.

This is perhaps the hardest lesson to share. Connect before you need to, and be patient with the process. Just the simple fact of reaching out two to three times a year will put you in good standing with another.

BEING A GOOD CONNECTOR

Let's rate yourself on each of the 10 Characteristics of a Good Connector.

Characteristic	My Rating Rate your competence on a scale of 0–10.
1. Connectors feel good about themselves. They walk into a room with their heads held high, and they tell themselves they have as much right to be there as everyone else.	Not at All 0 1 2 3 4 5 6 7 8 A lot

2. Good connectors are organized. They plan and prepare before attending events. They don't just show up. • YOUTRY prepared • cards in pocket and index cards ready • questions prepared They know: • who is going to be there • how they are going to get there...and back • who the host of the event is • who their wingpersons will be • which dress/suit they will wear • when it starts and ends	**Not at All 0 1 2 3 4 5 6 7 8 A lot**
3. Good connectors smile, even if other people look scared. They are respectful to everyone.	**Not at All 0 1 2 3 4 5 6 7 8 A lot**
4. Good connectors have great listening skills. They listen and give their full attention. They show genuine interest.	**Not at All 0 1 2 3 4 5 6 7 8 A lot**
5. Good connectors follow up. They use follow-up Fridays to conduct all outreach activities to their six/seven/$uccess cohorts.	**Not at All 0 1 2 3 4 5 6 7 8 A lot**

6. Good connectors have goals for the number of people they plan to meet, and they are persistent when they spot opportunities.	**Not at All 0 1 2 3 4 5 6 7 8 A lot**
7. Good connectors ask the right questions.	**Not at All 0 1 2 3 4 5 6 7 8 A lot**
8. Good connectors introduce others.	**Not at All 0 1 2 3 4 5 6 7 8 A lot**
9. Good connectors introduce others. They know how to play host.	**Not at All 0 1 2 3 4 5 6 7 8 A lot**
10. Good connectors know when it's time to leave the conversation and move on.	**Not at All 0 1 2 3 4 5 6 7 8 A lot**

Is this something most people do? Why? Why not?

Learn from the Masters

This is a great activity to use with connects. Find people in your network who are master connectors, and ask them for some advice about each of the above area. They will be thoroughly impressed by your effort to make connections, and it will increase their confidence in you. It will show them that you are developing good skills, and it will help increase their confidence in referring you to a friend or colleague. Ask connects to rate you using the connect matrix. Your wingperson can do the same.

COMMUNICATING WITH YOUR CONNECT

"While we know it's possible to reach others; our concern should be whether others can reach us."

~ Edward DeJesus

Your skill as a connector is getting people to like you. And it's not as easy as it sounds. In the long run, it is not only what you know or who you know; it's who knows and likes you that makes the difference. So what are the strategies to get people not only to like you but to help you? We'll talk about two things: credibility and rapport.

Credibility is the believability of your message. Rapport is the establishment of mutual trust and respect. If you are serious about building your social capital, you must develop both. You must make every effort to walk the walk and not only talk the talk. A connect can smell someone looking to get a reference a mile away. Expecting a reference letter, help getting a job, or an introduction to a new contact without first establishing credibility and rapport is a big mistake.

Once you establish credibility, rapport can follow. Rapport doesn't happen immediately. It takes time. That's why we developed the six/seven/$uccess plan. We don't want you to see connecting as a one-time event. You must make an effort to build rapport with your connect long before you need any type of assistance.

Credibility comes from presenting clear evidence that you are truly committed to your FEO goals. The way to establish credibility is simple:

1. Tell your connect the active steps you took in the past few weeks to build your FEO. Be concise. People want to hear your plan.

2. Show your connect evidence of the steps you are taking to make your goals a reality. Give your connect convincing evidence that you are making progress on your FEO (certificates, degrees, enrollment letters, photographs, videos, etc.). For example, if you want to convince a connect that you have pursued your education, send a copy of your most recent progress report. If you have been looking for work, mention where you have applied for a job. A registration confirmation, a recent report card, or a business card from someone the connect recommended are a few ways to show you're serious about your future.

3. Call on others to support your claims. It's not a bad idea to have a parent, teacher, or friend speak out on your behalf. Use other connects in the process.

4. Admit your challenges. Be honest about your setbacks, and be prepared to show how you corrected yourself and are moving forward.

Once you've established baseline credibility, you can start working on rapport. Here are some simple recommendations to help you build it.

1. Find Common Ground
   How many times have you seen two people connect just because they went to the same school, lived in the same neighborhood, or played the same sport? Even if these things didn't occur at the same time, people

always react with glee when they meet someone with similar experiences—that's a form a rapport. When you meet someone new, do your best to find something you have in common. Use open-ended questions to discover personal information about the person. Perhaps you attended the same school, lived on the same block, or know a common person. Use your connection questions to build common ground.

2. Dress Neutrally
   Your attire can say so much about you. People make judgments about how people dress. When trying to build rapport, always dress neutrally so your connect can focus on you and not on what you're wearing.

3. Maintain Good Body Language
   Poor posture can be a sign of a lack of confidence. Connects want to know that you are ready for the task even if you have to fake it. Watch out for distractions like tapping your foot, chewing gum, or glancing around. You will appear rude.

4. Don't Overuse Cologne or Perfume
   Avoid putting on too much cologne or perfume. While you want to smell nice, you don't want your fragrance to irritate others. Showering the day of and putting on deodorant are adequate.

5. Cell Phones
   No vibrating phones; text messaging; or, even worse, answering calls when you are with a connect. There is no greater connection killer than a ringing or buzzing cell phone. While you are connecting, make sure you turn your phone on silent. *Do not turn it off.* You may want to record someone's contact information on your phone or have someone take a picture of the both of you to send a card or e-mail. But do whatever it takes to silence your phone before you meet with a connect.

The Mirror Test

A great way to help prepare for connection events is to do the mirror test. You don't need a mirror. All you have to do is answer the following questions: how do you look from twelve feet away? How are you sensed form twelve inches away? What will be the first six words out of your mouth?

I am wearing black dress pants; a white, button-down shirt; black socks; and black dress shoes. I am smiling, holding my head up, and walking toward my connect with my hands slightly extended for a great shake. When I met her I say: Hello, my name is John Smith.

How do you look from twelve feet away?

_____
_____
_____

How are you sensed form twelve inches away?

_____
_____
_____

What will be the first six words out of your mouth?

_____
_____
_____

As you go through the mirror exercise, ask yourself what is missing.

If you are missing anything, take time to acquire that item or spend time mastering that behavior. If it's a behavior, such as giving a firm handshake while looking the connect in the eye, then practice, practice, practice. You may need to work on that smile—practice. You may see yourself extending a business card, but you don't have one. Make one. You see yourself receiving the person's business card, but you don't have a place to put it. Ask for a business-card holder for Christmas. If you work these things out beforehand, the connection will be easy, and you will be more confident. As long as you practice, you should be ready for any connecting opportunity.

Connectors get extremely nervous when presented with connecting opportunities because they haven't properly prepared. The art of connecting is just that—art. Have you ever witnessed people who flow easily in and out of conversations? Are they superhuman? No. They probably use the same lines over and over again. Years and years of practice have enabled them to sail in and out of conversations like a ship on smooth seas. Mastering your YOUTRY statements will help.

Below, we provide you with a list of more than twenty questions. Choose five that you think are most relevant to your situation and *own* them. These are the main questions that you will use when connecting.

Powerful, Connecting Questions

What do you like best about what you do?

What got you started in that industry/career/line of work?

What are some of your biggest challenges in hiring new people?

How did you get involved in…?

What made you decide to major in…?

What made you decide to attend (name of school)?

What made you decide to go into the ___ business?

How did you get your start in the ___ business?

What advice would you give someone just starting in this business/profession/major?

What do you love/enjoy most about your business/ profession/major?

What separates you from the competition?

What separates your business/company/organization from the competition?

What one thing would you do if you knew you couldn't fail?

What one thing would you do with your business if you knew that you couldn't fail?

What one thing would you do if you knew you were guaranteed to succeed?

What was the strangest or funniest incident you've experienced in your business/at your school/in your organization?

What significant changes have you seen take place in your profession/area of expertise/school/major through the years?

What do you see as the coming trends in your profession/area of expertise?

How do think education will be different in the future?

What do you see as the coming trends in your business?

What do you think will change about your industry in the future?

How would someone describe you in one sentence?

How would someone describe your business/company/school in one sentence?

What ways have you found to be the most effective for promoting your business/organization/product?

It's the end of a great week, and you have some free time on your hands—what would you do?

What would make someone the ideal employee (or intern) for your company or organization?

Practice, practice, practice. It is the only way to master communication. As social-capital builders, we drill students on their YOUTRY statements until they can recite them without looking at the paper. Also, we have contests for those with the best statements and delivery. Business executives spend thousands of dollars in training programs just to master their three-minute elevator speech. Spending twenty-six minutes a day for a few days developing this skill is well worth the investment.

Hey, why don't you put your statement on the back of your business card? It would be a great way for your connect to remember you. Just an idea!
You can post your YOUTRY statement on your social-media pages, make flyers, and distribute them out at family events. Do whatever works to help your network learn about your goals and aspirations. As stated numerous times throughout this book, no matter what religion, race, or orientation, adults want to help young people who are trying to make it. Use that power to your advantage, and get connected now.

Leaving the Conversation

You did a great job. You successfully approached a potential connect, greeted him or her, and delivered your YOUTRY statement. You initiated great listening skills, smiles, and handshakes. You got the connect's attention, and he or she seemed impressed by you. You asked for the connect's business card and jotted down pertinent information on your MCW five-by-seven cards. Now what? You feel anxious about leaving the safety of this connection. After all, who wants to go through this again? Moreover, you don't want to appear rude or crass. You would hate the person to think that you are disrespectful.

Here's another scenario. You are at a connection event, meeting some really cool people. You find yourself talking to a person who won't stop talking and is not at all helpful to you. You want to exit stage left but don't know how.

The answer is simple—have an exit strategy. An exit strategy is extremely important and a big part of connecting. Remember, you have more contacts to make. In our process, shoot to make at least three connections at each connecting opportunity.

For many people (including master connectors), learning how to enter into a conversation and how to end it properly are equally important tasks. Exit a conversation by asking the person to help you meet other people. Be honest and let the connect know you're trying to make more connections. Blame it on the program.

Here's an example of how to leave gracefully.
"It was a pleasure meeting you, and I look forward to following up. I'm going to circulate and meet some more people. I need to see three more people to complete my assignment. I just joined the Making Connections Work program to learn how to connect. Is there anyone else here you suggest I speak with?"

Connection Checklist

___ Carry business cards.

___ Meet at least six people at each networking event.

___ Spend no more than ten minutes with each person.

___ Leave graciously.

___ Be prepared to share something.

Fake It Till You Make It

Now that you are comfortable with what to say, make sure you're comfortable with how you look. We aren't talking only about attire. We're talking about looking the part. So much of your energy is in what we call your state. Let's say you just heard some bad news; do you think connect will be able to tell the state you're in? We think so. We can't control the things that happen around us, but we can control the state we're in. Will you appear joyous and happy, or will you appear sullen and scared?

Put on your game face. Fake it till you make it. You will be uncomfortable at the start of the event, but the discomfort will quickly pass. You'll probably become the talk of the town. People will admire your youth and vigilance. You will be one of the few people who was properly trained in our process. The truth is, most people have never gone through this type of training and do not have a tenth of the degree of preparation that you'll have. If you see any of those people standing alone in the corner, go up to them. Give them your YOUTRY statement, and ask them if they would like to join you in meeting people.

Get in the right state! Let go of any feelings of insecurity or unworthiness. You have the right to opportunity and the best life you can have. You have the right to build your social capital. It costs nothing and takes away from no one. In fact, it will be a shame if people never have the opportunity to meet you. Think of everyone at the event as a timid, unsure person who needs your help. Then help. You must go confidently to each event with this mind-set. It's the same when meeting with a connect. You want to show that you have the confidence and self-esteem that will make you a star.

At a recent MCW training, we were explaining the MCW process and the importance of building social capital. One young woman, a recent community-college graduate, started crying. We were thrown off. What did we say that affected her so?

We took her into the hall so we could talk and asked her what was wrong. She shared with us that she had been in foster care for most of her life. Most of the adults in her life abandoned her. She didn't believe people were out there who wanted to help.

While this may be an extreme case, internal negative emotions or false assumptions are what hold most people back from making connections. Connections can radically change your life. Similarly, in our work with at-risk youth, they constantly complain, "I don't know that person like that." What do they mean? If someone is not from their neighborhood or is not a family member, then there is no reason to connect? It's an insidious mind-set that undermines opportunity for many young people who desperately need options beyond the streets.

Your success in building connections is partly based on your mental outlook. If you think that no one wants to help, then no one will. Even if someone does, you won't see it as help, and you will alienate the person who is trying.

During a recent discussion with a group of MCW trainers in Washington, DC, we spoke about helping students change their negative mind-sets about making connections. One young trainer said, "There's not much to be positive about right now. Jobs are scarce, and competition is intense. With all the competition, people are holding information about jobs and other opportunities close to the vest. At least that's what young people think."

We once again directed the group to our opening exercise. "The fact that 47 percent of people find jobs through connections has held consistent every year for the past five years. That means someone is doing it, and it's working. It's just not the young people we serve. They've never been taught."

We asked them to think about what might change if instead of saying, "Nobody wants to help," young people asked, "Who do I know who was helped?"

Who got help finding a job?
Who got help graduating from school?

Who got help finding a scholarship?

The answer will likely be someone who was well-connected and used those connections to obtain opportunity. With a simple question, you can drastically change your mind-set. Instead of feeling that people are not amenable to helping, recognize the people around you who are being helped every day. If you work with the power of making and sustaining connections, you will unleash the power that is already within your reach.

CHAPTER FOURTEEN

WRITING TO YOUR CONNECT

"You never know when a moment and a few sincere words can have an impact on a life."

~Zig Ziglar

Much of connecting never takes place person to person or over the phone. Your interactions will likely happen through written communication, usually an e-mail note or a thank-you card. Regardless of the type of written correspondence you use, it is a great tool to build relationships.

Becoming a better writer means you must become a better reader. As you gain experience reading a variety of materials, you will increasingly try to spell words by using patterns you have seen in print. The best way to become more comfortable with writing is to read. Many websites guide you through formatting a proper business letter or note. Below are some excellent books that will help you become a better writer as well increase your connecting skills.

1. *How to Win Friends and Influence People* by Dale Carnegie
2. *The Pocket Style Manual* by Diana Hacker and Nancy Sommers
3. *Think and Grow Rich* by Napoleon Hill
4. *Business Writing for Dummies* by Natalie Canavo
5. *The Elements of Style* by William Strunk Jr. and E. B. White.

6. *Power of Your Spoken Word* by Louise Hay
7. *Awaken the Giant Within* by Anthony Robbins
8. *The Sense of Style: The Thinking Person's Guide to Writing in the 21st Century*, by Stephen Pinker
9. *How to Say It: Choice Words, Phrases, Sentences, and Paragraphs for Every Situation, Rosalie Maggio*
10. *Prompting* by Kody Bateman

On Writing Good Notes

You might not be confident in your writing ability. A good way to build your writing skills is to write your letters in advance and have someone, preferably a good writer, review them. The goal is to have a series of different notes and letters handy that only require minimal edits and changes.

There are many forms of written correspondence that you can use when "touching" connects. You can alter a general note to fit a variety of circumstances. It largely depends on the particular reason and occasion. For example:

- When referring another connect, send an e-mail;
- On a connect's birthday, send a birthday card;
- When a connect has an upcoming event, send a good-luck e-mail.

Let's take a look at the benefits of a simple thank-you note:

1. The thank-you note shows your commitment to respect and value. It articulates a clear interest in building a relationship and a willingness to place effort in it. It is evidence that you are willing to go the extra mile, take the extra step to get the job done.

2. The thank-you note is a writing sample. It demonstrates good communication skills. Make sure your thoughts are clear and that your language is

appropriate and grammar correct.

3. The thank-you note provides you an easy opportunity to continue the conversation, show your connect that you are serious, and provide evidence that you are someone who gets the job done. When connects extends their hands to help, they want to know that they aren't wasting time. They want to know that you will act on their advice and recommendations. Sending a follow-up note is proof that you are that type of person.

4. The thank-you note is a reminder of who you are and why you met. Connects are often busy and may have forgotten to follow up on your behalf. Any good salesperson knows that with every additional "touch point," your chances of selling increase.

5. When you use the thank-you note as a relationship-building tool; you will be seen as a person worth knowing and with whom people want to work. Most importantly, it will help you build your writing skills. You become a better writer by writing. Given the number of connects in your six/seven/$uccess plan, you should be a master writer by the end of this course.

How to Write an Effective Note

Date:

Contact Name (only use when writing a formal letter):
Title:

Company Address:

City, State, Zip:

1. *Greeting:*
2. *Introduce/reference yourself:*
3. *Thank your contact for his or her consideration, update on your progress, congratulate him or her on an accomplishment, and so on:*
4. *Explain why you are writing:*
5. *Explain your next step:*
6. *Always add your telephone number or e-mail address, in case the contact wants to get back to you:*

Remember:

- Be brief.
- Be positive.
- Be organized.

Referred by a Strong-Tie—Sample Letter

Date
Contact Name
Title
Company
Address
City, State, Zip

Dear Mr./Ms. Contact,

I was referred to you by Ms. White from the People's Health Exchange. She recommended you as an excellent source of information on the health-care industry.

My goal is to secure an entry-level position in the health-care field. I would appreciate hearing your advice on career opportunities in the industry, necessary credentials, and how best to uncover job leads.

Thanks so much, in advance, for any insight and advice you would be willing to share. I look forward to contacting you early next week to set up a telephone informational interview.

Thank you for your consideration.

Sincerely,

Your First and Last Name
Phone number

Sample Follow-Up E-mails

Sample A:

Dear Mr. Diaz:

I enjoyed our conversation last Tuesday at the Ceres Chamber of Commerce breakfast. Thanks for taking the time to speak with me about careers in health care.

I wanted to let you know that I followed up with your suggestion. I signed up for CPR/First-Aid training. Classes start on March fifteenth.

I'm looking forward to a great career helping others. Thanks for helping me.

Sincerely,

Marco Quintana
555-222-3333

Sample B:

January 15, 2017

Dear Mr. Diaz:

It has been two months since we met at the Ceres Chamber of Commerce breakfast. Thanks for taking the time to speak to me about careers in health care.

I took a look at my calendar and realized that today is your birthday. Happy birthday! I wish you all the health and happiness in the world.

I also wanted to let you know that I started my CPR class today.

Enjoy your day, and I look forward to meeting you again.

Sincerely,
Marco Quintana
Project YES
555-222-3333

Your Turn:

_____

_____:

_____

_____.

_____

_____

_____.

_____

_____.

_____,

_____

_____

_____

Verbal Communication

Below are verbal-communication tips that you should strive to master. By improving your verbal-communication skills, you will quickly connect and build rapport, earn respect, gain influence, and become more likable and accepted.

Smile. It's simple. Don't walk around with a mean face. People will warm up to you if you are smiling. They might run if you look angry.

Be friendly by shaking hands. A handshake and a smile go a long way. Effective communicators know that this gives them the edge. People are drawn to others who make the feel good about themselves. Don't let others think that communicating with you will be an arduous task. Set the tone on how easy it will be by shaking hands and smiling.

Use your YOUTRY Statement.

Have someone introduce you. In our program, you will never connect alone. There should be a wingperson at all connecting events. Ask your wingperson to introduce you to specific people. Don't be shy.

Ask a question. When you join a group or enter into a conversation, use what you were taught. Deliver your YOUTRY statement. You should have practiced this statement one hundred times by now. Use it! People love to hear from young people working to improve their lives.

Show you're listening to nonverbal clues. People love to talk about themselves. Open them up, and let them go. A great smile and handshake is the door opener. Let them invite you in by just asking follow-up questions: Tell me more about that. How did it make you feel? Listen with great interest, and you will be amazed by how much people share.

Be prepared. Have your MCW card, business cards, pens, and your phone available to record contact information and notes.

People like to hear their own names. Use the person's name at least three times during the conversation. This is a great way to help you remember. Also write down any important facts about the person on your MCW card.

Be clear. Connects don't have the time and don't want to spend energy trying to figure out what you're trying to say. Don't be indirect or go on about your day. Show respect to your connect by saying what you mean and meaning what you say. When there is something you want to say, ask yourself, "Is this the clearest way I can communicate?"

Speak so they can hear you. Yeah, that means you!

Don't talk too much. Don't speak for more than thirty seconds. Few people like to be around a chatterbox. Let them ask you questions, and be prepared to give great answers.

Show confidence. The words you choose, your tone, eye contact, and body language all reflect confidence. Choose wisely.

The Test

Out loud, answer the following question in five complete sentences, without using any ums, ahs, and ands!

Why are you at this opportunity event?

Why should I be your connect?

On index cards, list common conversation subjects. Place the index cards in a box. Alternating between you and a friend, pick a card from the box and speak for thirty seconds on the subject.

- weather
- favorite sports team
- the city you're in
- best movie of the year
- old-school music
- current event

You are at an opportunity event for the local business association. You see the nametag of someone who works at the local hospital. You are interested in an entry-level job in health care. Using the criteria listed on the speaking with your Connect worksheet, approach the person, and make a connection.

STAYING CREDIBLE AND VISIBLE

While most people know that follow-up is important, few are masterful at it. Leaving one or two voicemails or sending a couple of e-mails is only a small part of what follow-up is all about.

Staying in contact with a connect is about survival. Your career success will likely have more to do with who you know than what you know. Forgetting to stay in contact with those who helped you can be economic suicide.

Staying in contact with your connect is not about nagging or harassing. It's about reminding. Remind people of the wonderful, valuable ways that they have helped. Follow-up is acknowledgment, and people like to be acknowledged. Smart connectors know that recognizing people makes them more receptive. By definition, receptive people are always ready to help.

What do you think credibility means? We like to define credibility as the believability of a source or message. Basically, credibility is the connect's assessment of the believability of the connector. To put it simply, people will do things for you if they believe in you. It's your job to make them believe.

There is a credibility problem in the United States, and we don't want you to be a part of it. In today's world of instant communication and lightning speed decision-making, establishing your credibility is becoming more challenging.

But it drives people's attitude and, ultimately, what they believe and feel about you.

According to the 2013 Edelman Trust Survey, only 38 percent of the population trust business to do what is right, and 75 percent feel that companies don't tell the truth in advertising. Many bloggers are now more credible with the public than major news outlets.

So what can you do about your credibility? Remember that every personal and business interaction is an opportunity to establish and build your credibility. Take advantage of every one of those interactions by preparing ahead of time.

At Social Capital Builders, we know that the best way to establish credibility with your connect is to demonstrate your commitment to your FEO. We call these FEO commitments. There is no stronger builder of credibility than watching a young person take action on his or her goals. To establish credibility, you should focus on:

- Telling—Make connects believe and trust what you say. Tell them what active steps you took in the past few weeks to build your FEO. This gives your message credibility, plus connects always like to hear what steps people are taking to improve their lives.
- Showing—Back up your statements with compelling evidence. Give your connects convincing evidence that you are making progress in your FEO (certificates, degrees, enrollment letters, photographs, videos, etc.). For example, if you want to convince a connect that you have been pursuing your education, send them a copy of your most recent progress report. If you have been looking for work, mention the places where you have applied for a job.
- Calling—Call on others to back up your claims.
- Admitting—Be honest about your setbacks, and be

prepared to show how you corrected yourself and are moving forward.

GET TO WORK

In each circle in the box below, list what you have done in the past eight weeks to build each area of FEO.

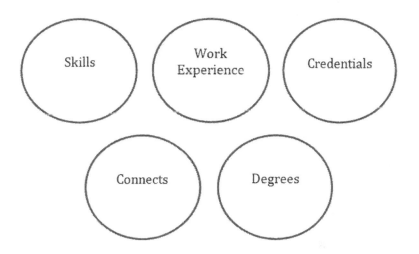

Below, list other ways to demonstrate good FEO evidence.

Ways to Build FEO Evidence

1. _____

2. _____

3. _____

4. _____

5. _____

**Connection Corner,
Becky, Age 25**

For three years, she was right there, always at rehearsal practice, volunteering as a choir assistant. She had the most beautiful voice and the most pleasant personality. She always encouraged me to follow my dream to be a talk-show host. She never spoke an unkind word. Five years later, I'm looking for a job in television production, and I see her on TV as the local news anchor. I wanted to kick myself. I should have stayed in contact.

Losing contact with people is an inevitable part of life, and we all regret losing contact with someone from our lives. How often have you heard stories of someone losing contact with someone who later became a major power player in business, entertainment, sports, or politics? Stories abound of these types of missed opportunities. You may have had a direct connection to the president of a major corporation, but you never followed up or stayed in contact. Now, several years later, you are in need of a connection to that company in order to close a major sales deal that could radically transform your life.

It often happens because many people do not practice the art of making connections. Most of us weren't taught these skills in school or at home and were not provided the resources and opportunities to develop them.

It only takes two to three contacts per year with someone for that person to say you are part of his or her network. We aren't talking about Facebook friends. We are talking about people whom you have had a direct one-to-one conversation with by mail, phone, and in person. It only takes two contacts a year!

If you have lost contact with someone, and it has been years, the good news is that you can get the contact back. You must act now, and build that connection long before you need it. If you desperately need it now, you're going to have to wait at least a month after initiating the six/seven/$uccess plan before you can make a formal request for assistance. Remember, it is all about building the relationship well before you need anything. Don't fall into the same situation again. You have completed a list of touches—start touching. Follow the plan, and the plan will work for you. If you do nothing, you will achieve nothing.

Let's get to work.

It's all about being prepared. You can use the following script when contacting connects to update them on your progress and give that FEO evidence:

Hello, _____, this is _____ calling. How are you?

I am calling to thank you for your help. I just wanted to let you know that I really appreciated all you've done for me and I wanted to update you on my progress. Do you have a minute?

In the past few months/years, I have (your demonstrated FEO commitments) :

1. _____

_____

2. _____

_____

I really wanted to share this with you since you were a big part of my success. Well, that's it. I just wanted to let you know.

Thanks Again!

Chapter Fifteen

CONCLUSION—WELCOME TO THE CONNECTIUM

"In the long history of humankind, those who learned to collaborate and improvise most effectively have prevailed."
~ Charles Darwin

The economy is changing in ways that no one anticipated. Half of the jobs that will be available in the next ten years haven't been identified yet. The Department of Labor will be the first to admit that it cannot confidently predict future workforce changes. Changes brought about by e-commerce and the Internet have changed the labor landscape. To be prepared, your best option is to be well-connected. If not, you run the risk being of being left behind even after you secure a solid foothold.

We are all connected. You are too. We call it "the connectium." We define it as an identifiable set of connections characterized by mutual interests, ideas, places, or people. We all live in it, but 98 percent of the population is unaware it exists. Every time something positive manifests in your life—when you get a job, find out about a scholarship, or gain access to a great opportunity—it is usually because of the connectium. The connectium is always there, and we were already connected. It's like having the power on, the lamp plugged in, and never turning it on.

The day you were born, your parents passed on hundreds of connections to you. Each year of your life, your connections increased exponentially. Each person your parents, friends,

Connection Corner, Janae, Age 22

I first started making connections my sophomore year of college. I wasn't even aware that what I was building social capital until later on. I knew I was passionate about acting and dancing and wanted to get involved in as many projects as possible. I was a theater and dance major in college and developed a strong liking for film acting toward the end of my freshman year. The first film I was involved with, I talked to as many people behind the scenes as I could; not just my fellow actors but the crew as well. Over time, all of the projects I have been involved with have led me to make many friendships and connections. I keep in touch with as many of them as possible. I send invitations to casting directors I've met and fellow actors whenever I'm on a show. Social media is a great way to stay connected. They get to see posts of everything I'm involved with and vice-versa.

and coworkers meet is part of the connectium. They are your social capital.

If you want to improve your chances of landing a good internship or job, invest some of your family's hard-earned social capital. Do you know how much you have? Research states that you probably know 611 people who also know 611 people—that's 373,321 people in your network. Somewhere in that large network are many who are ready to lend a hand. So what are you waiting for? Let's put these connections to work.

At your fingertips, you already have access to all the information that you need about job opportunities, scholarships, and affordable housing to make sure you build a solid future. You already know the person who is going to help you get your next job. Act like it.

That's why we wrote *Making Connections Work*. We wanted to develop a way to help you invest your valuable social capital. We call it six/seven/$uccess.

There's no room for failure when it comes to your future. For far too long, schools have not taught the number-one skill for getting jobs, building careers, and making connections to opportunities. It's time to start.

Our wish for you is that you discover your place in the connectium and work to manifest the social capital that's your birthright. The power is on, and all you have to do is turn on the switch.

Make your connections work.

NOTES

McCormick TH, Salganik MJ, Zheng T. How many people do you know?: Efficiently estimating personal network size. Journal of the American Statistical Association. 2010;105(489):59-70. doi:10.1198/jasa.2009.ap08518.

Granovetter, M. S. (1995). Getting a job: A study of contacts and careers. Chicago: University of Chicago Press.

Sullivan, D. J. (2015, July 23). 10 Compelling Numbers That Reveal the Power of Employee Referrals. Retrieved March 25, 2017, from https://www.eremedia.com/ere/10-compelling-numbers-that-reveal-the-power-of-employee-referrals/

Sandra Smith and Kara Young. (2013). "Why Blue-Collar Blacks Help Less." IRLE Working Paper No. 139-13. http://irle.berkeley.edu/workingpapers/139-13.pdf

Lesser, E. L. (2011). Knowledge and Social Capital. Elsevier Science & Technology.

Rick, Scott and Schweitzer, Maurice E., The Imbibing Idiot Bias: Consuming Alcohol Can Be Hazardous to Your (Perceived) Intelligence (June 12, 2012). Forthcoming, *Journal of Consumer Psychology*. Available at SSRN: https://ssrn.com/abstract=1623056 or http://dx.doi.org/10.2139/ssrn.1623056

Number of Employers Using Social Media to Screen Candidates Has Increased 500 Percent over the Last Decade. (n.d.). Retrieved March 25, 2017, from http://www.careerbuilder.com/share/aboutus/pressreleasesdetail.aspx?ed=12%2F31%2F2016&id=pr945&sd=4%2F28%2F2016, CareerBuilder's annual social media recruitment survey

Mulvey, T. (2013, April 10). SHRM Survey Findings: Social Networking Websites and Recruiting/Selec... Retrieved March 25, 2017, from http://www.slideshare.net/shrm/social-networkingwebsitesrecruitingselectingjobcandidatesshrm2013final, Society for Human Resource Management

Associated Press. (2012, April 23). Half of recent college grads underemployed or jobless, analysis says [Press release]. Retrieved from http://www.cleveland.com/business/index.ssf/2012/04/half_of_recent_college_grads_u.html

U.S. Department of Education, National Center for Education Statistics. (2016). The Condition of Education 2016 (NCES 2016-144), Undergraduate Retention and Graduation Rates.

About The Authors

Keith Hosea

Keith is the president of Telios Training Solutions. He is a well-known motivational speaker and a dedicated youth advocate. His rare talent as a public speaker, his passion for lifelong learning, and his unique blend of wit and wisdom have made him an audience favorite at conferences, seminars, and workshops all around the country. Over the last two decades, his focus has been on serving the prolific population of current and former foster youth throughout the state of California.

Joseph Williams

Joseph is the founder and CEO of the Youth Action Project (YAP) and has served youth and adults of the Inland Empire for the past fourteen years. Joseph has twenty years' experience empowering youth and adults through workforce and education innovation initiatives. He serves as a governor's appointee to two state workforce-development policy-making bodies and is the president of a local community college board of trustees. Joseph is finishing his masters of arts in social impact and believes that *Making Connections Work* will be one of the keys that unlock the door of success for all readers.

Edward DeJesus

Ed is the founder of Social Capital Builders. He is a top speaker at over thirty major youth conferences and events each year. He is the author of the best-selling book, *MAKiN' iT* as well as the author of several publications on issues affecting marginalized young adults. Ed is a W. K. Kellogg Foundation fellow, a father of six, and a competitive ironman triathlete.

Notes

Notes

MAKING CONNECTIONS WORK ORDER FORM

MAKING CONNECTIONS WORK

by Keith Hosea, Joseph Williams and Edward DeJesus

EDSC
EDWARD DeJESUS SEMINARS & CONSULTING

The #1 Skill for 21st Century Workforce Success

"Making Connections Work (MCW) gives both young and older workers a solid plan to build their "connecting" or networking skills and an innovative strategy to implement them, providing a key to open the door to the hidden labor market and the plethora of opportunities behind it."

-Van Ton-Quinlivan, Vice ChancellorWorkforce & Economic Development Division , California Community College

Please make check payable to EDSC
mail to:
EDSC, 267 Kentlands Boulevard, #5094
Gaithersburg, MD 20878 or email form to
ed@socialcapitalbuillders.com
www.mcwbook.com

Shipping info:
Name:

Address:

City: _____ State: _____ Zip: _____

Phone: _____ e-mail: _____

Billing Info:
Name on Card

Billing Address

Card Number

Exp: Date _____ , Sec Code _____

Item	Quantity	Unit Price	Total
MAKING CONNECTIONS WORK		$14.95	
MAKING CONNECTIONS WORK (Bulk 50 plus copies)		$10.00	
HANDBOOK		$24.95	
CURRICULUM		$299.50	
Tax id: 83-0348662		Shipping/Handling (5% or min $6.99, whichever is greater)	
		TOTAL	

159

Bring a Making Connections Work Seminar to Your Organization

Thousands of others have employed the Making Connections Work strategy to help connect their students to work and education. You can too.

Bring a Making Connections Work seminar to your organization/school/community. Teach youth the importance of building social capital and help them acquire the #1 skill for workforce and career success.

Find out more at
www.socialcapitalbuilders.com

Building connections is the key to workforce and entrepreneurial success. Regrettably, 90% of schools do not offer formal programs or resources to help students do so. In this book, you will learn the secrets to getting a job and moving in the world of work. You will get the keys to unlock the hidden job market and secure connections to the nebulae of networks were most careers are born.

"Making Connections Work is an insightful, engaging, and refreshing book that examines what is necessary for youth and young adults to be successful in life. Comprehensive in its scope, the authors do a superb job of coupling theory with practice. The examples integrated throughout the book are practical and useful. The importance of communication is at the core of the book's message. This book is an excellent manual on how the power of networking increases upward mobility. Indeed, it is a must read for those who want to understand the strategies that lead to success—and greatness."
Renford Reese, Ph.D., Founder/Director, Reintegration Academy

"Not only is the economy changing, but the pace at which it evolves is also increasing. This rapid pace of change requires us to establish reskilling as the new norm for all generations, not just younger ones. Making Connections Work (MCW) gives both young and older workers a solid plan to build their "connecting" or networking skills and an innovative strategy to implement them, providing a key to open the door to the hidden labor market and the plethora of opportunities behind it."
-Van Ton-Quinlivan, Vice Chancellor Workforce & Economic Development Division Chancellor's Office, California Community College

"Making Connections Work (MCW) is a must read for all young adults interested in getting a job, building a care~~...~~ economic success."

www.socialcapitalbuilders.com

ISBN 9780692855980

90000 >

9 780692 855980